Mary Alphonsus Downing

Voices From the Heart

Sacred Poems

Mary Alphonsus Downing

Voices From the Heart
Sacred Poems

ISBN/EAN: 9783744713504

Printed in Europe, USA, Canada, Australia, Japan

Cover: Foto ©Thomas Meinert / pixelio.de

More available books at **www.hansebooks.com**

VOICES FROM THE HEART.

Sacred Poems

BY

SISTER MARY ALPHONSUS DOWNING,

Of the Third Order of Saint Dominic.

AUTHOR OF "MEDITATIONS AND PRAYERS IN HONOUR OF ST. CATHERINE OF SIENA, AND OTHER SAINTS."

NEW AND ENLARGED EDITION.

REVISED BY THE

RIGHT REV. DOCTOR LEAHY,

BISHOP OF DROMORE.

"Sing to the Lord a new song."—Ps. xcv.

DUBLIN:
M. H. GILL AND SON, 50 UPPER SACKVILLE-ST
1881.

Imprimatur:

✠ E. MAC CABE,

ARCHIEP. DUBLINENSIS,

ET PRIMAS HIBERN.

In Festo Purif. B.M.V., 1880.

PRINTED BY M. H. GILL & SON, 50 UPPER SACKVILLE-STREET, DUBLIN.

DEDICATION.

TO

Saint Alphonsus Maria de Liguori,

MY PATRON, FRIEND, AND GUIDE,

MY PHYSICIAN, AND MY FATHER,

WHOSE PEN HAS INSTRUCTED ME,

WHOSE LIFE HAS PLEADED FOR ME,

WHOSE PRAYERS HAVE SHELTERED ME,

WHO TAUGHT ME TO PRAY,

TO VISIT THE BLESSED SACRAMENT,

AND TO SEEK THE CRUCIFIED SON

THROUGH THE IMMACULATE MOTHER;

LOVINGLY, GRATEFULLY, AND REVERENTLY

I DEDICATE MY FIRST LITTLE BOOK.

MARY ALPHONSUS.

PREFACE.

MANY poems require neither commentary nor introduction. They explain themselves, and speak to the reader by their intrinsic beauty. Yet there are few that do not grow in interest when we know by whom, and in what circumstances they were composed; and occasionally the knowledge of such circumstances is necessary to clear up obscurity, or to bring out all the beauty of a poem. In the following collection of "VOICES FROM THE HEART," there are some, the full sense or pathos of which might be missed without some such word of introduction; and though the former edition (the first public one) appeared without a Preface, we know that the eagerness of many to possess the book was caused by their previous knowledge of the life of its Authoress.

The Rev. Matthew Russell, S.J., the accomplished editor of the *Irish Monthly*, in a series of five papers, which appeared in the year 1878, in the sixth annual volume of that Magazine, first made the general public acquainted with the outlines of the life of Miss Ellen Downing, whose poetic signature of "Mary" had been familiarly known to the readers of the *Nation*, and had been eagerly looked forward to in the years 1846-7, but who had almost passed from memory before she died, in the year 1869. Those who read the touching facts of the life which Father Russell so gracefully sketched, and the few extracts from her poems and letters which he gave, obtained a glimpse of a soul of so rare an excellence, that they longed to know more. In answer to this desire, a small volume of spiritual poems, which had been previously printed for private circulation, under the title of "Voices from the Heart," was given to the public in 1879. It was followed shortly after by a volume called "Meditations and Prayers," in which some fragments of prose, from the pen of Miss Downing, but left incomplete at her death, were gathered together. To this volume the Rev. Mother Mary Imelda, Prioress of the Dominican Convent of Saint Catherine of Siena, Drogheda, prefixed a memoir of her departed friend. It would not be easy to find a more perfect example of a spiritual biography. It was written by one who was not only intimately acquainted with the subject, but who had the deep insight conferred by kindred sanctity; and, being the history of one whose life had been a martyrdom of suffering, was composed amid the pangs of a last illness, and only completed a few days before death set the crown on a life of holy works. A short notice of the biographer, Mother Mary Imelda (in the world, Jane Eliza Magee), from the pen of the Bishop of Dromore, who had been her spiritual director, as well as of Sister Mary Alphonsus (Miss Downing), was prefixed to the Meditations, so that the memories of the two holy friends are enshrined together.

Miss Ellen Downing, then, had two other names by which she was better known to the world than by her own. Father Russell has treated of her principally as "Mary" of the *Nation*. Mother Mary Imelda has given fuller details of the latter part of her life, when she was known as Sister Mary Alphonsus, of the Third Order of Saint Dominic. The two biographies naturally complete each other. We cannot here reproduce them; we shall only draw from them such facts as may serve to clear up the few allusions in the poems, which might otherwise be obscure.

The first poem thus opens:—

> "Give me my early gift, and then
> No more for earth that gift shall be,—"

and there is in the whole poem a tone of remorse

which would startle and puzzle a reader unacquainted with the facts. She regrets that she can

> "never tell in song
> How much she mourns for all she said
> In praise of danger and of wrong:"

Again, at page 79, she exclaims :—

> "O my dear Lord! how was my wild youth wasted,
> Loved by a world that falsely spoke to me,
> Till each new hour, as far from me it hasted,
> Bore the new impress of some wrong to Thee."

What does all this mean? A reader totally unacquainted with the life of Sister Mary Alphonsus might ask if she were a convert from heresy or worldliness. No; the author of these words, truly "Voices from the Heart" though they be, was Catholic from her infant baptism. She acknowledges, with gratitude, at page 129,

> "My God! I am a Catholic, I grew into the ways
> Of Thy dear Church since first my voice could lisp a word of praise."

Piety grew up with her from her childhood. Her practical knowledge of "the world" was, perhaps, as small as has ever fallen to the lot of one who lived to middle age; and it is probable that no one, with an equally cultivated mind, has ever been more carefully and successfully trained in ignorance of the evil that can be learned in the world of literature. The explanation of her regrets is, that there were two periods or phases in the life of Miss Downing, and that "Mary" of the *Nation* was very different from Sister Mary Alphonsus. And though it may be hard for us to share her condemnation of the first period, we can cordially acknowledge how much it differed from, and fell short of, the second. In one of her poems, written at the age of seventeen, in a copy of Charles Lamb's Essays, on lending it to a friend, she charitably says:—

> "Wrong thoughts that in thy pages live
> My grateful pity can forgive;
> Wrong morals that may hither stray
> I do but weep and wish away."

There are no "wrong morals," in the ordinary sense of the word, in the writings of "Mary" of the *Nation*, to wish away, though there are some rather wild politics. But the political judgment of a young lady of eighteen can hardly be very mature. If at a later period she regretted "all she had said in praise of danger and of wrong," she seems to have been still more penitent for having given the first fruits of her intellect and heart to human love. Not that she ever wrote a word unworthy of a Christian maiden. But any one who reads the poems in the present volume, will see that the consecrated bride of Jesus Christ loved her Divine Spouse with so passionate a love that she could not but regret that her heart had not been all His from the beginning

When a novice in the North Presentation Convent in Cork, in the year 1850, at the age of twenty-two, she wrote a paper intended for the eye of God only, but which has been fortunately preserved. In this she says; "When I came first to Your feet, I wept continually over the fresh youth, the fervent spirit, that I had poured out upon the world. I wanted them back again for You; but I would be ashamed now to offer You so poor a gift; no, no, I never loved anything as I desire to love You."

The main facts of Miss Downing's life may be related in a few words. She was born at Cork, on the 19th March, 1828. Her father was, at the time of her birth, the resident medical officer of the Cork Fever Hospital. He was carried off, in the autumn of 1845, by fever, caught in the fulfilment of his perilous duties during an epidemic. Before his death, his daughter Ellen had already contributed verses to the *Nation* newspaper which gave proof of much poetic talent. For the next three years poetry and patriotism, or patriotism finding expression in poetry, absorbed her whole soul. She threw herself into the Young Ireland movement with all the energy of her being. Let the reader turn to the poem, at page 194, for the conversion of England. This most touching and Christian prayer has a far higher pathos and beauty when we know that it was a voice from the heart of one who had written to a friend in 1847: "If I get toothache here, it is through means of those English, clenching my teeth when I think of them, and look at the country they have darkened. I wasn't a patriot truly till now; but this blessed day I make an internal vow, and, please goodness, I'll keep it." This is expressed playfully, but it came from intense feeling. What was the nature of the vow may be guessed from her poems which at that time sing of arms and revenge. This she bitterly regretted afterwards. Of this period of her life, and of its climax and of the events which wrought this change, one of her biographers thus writes: "It is enough to say that she gave herself heart and soul to the cause in which she had implicit faith; wrote for it, worked for it, exhausted for it her feeble frame, buoyed up always by an enthusiastic but mistaken hope, amounting to certainty of success. All the early part of 1848 was passed by her in a fever of political excitement, and her delusive hopes were worked up to the very highest pitch, when, in the autumn of the same year, the blow fell, which in a few hours dashed them all to the ground. She was in the steamboat on the river, with her sister and brother-in-law, when the news reached her that John Mitchell was arrested, and the *United Irishman* suppressed. The shock was awful to her. Her brother-in-law took a car at Passage, and brought her home, as we are told, more dead than alive. Events followed each other in quick succession; in one week all her dearest friends were in prison. For days and weeks she lay in such a state of utter physical prostration that it was thought her life would pay the penalty of her mental anguish. But the God of all compassion, who would not break the bruised reed, and who had great designs upon her soul, came to her aid. When she afterwards wrote that 'the time of suffering is the time of grace—the advent of God,' she was but expressing her own experience." Sister Mary Alphonsus alludes to this epoch, when she writes at page 18 of this volume:—

> "I thank Thee, Lord, for all the pains
> That wrenched this trembling heart within;
> I bless the hand that broke the chains
> Which bound me to this world of sin."

It seems to have been during the long illness, brought on by the catastrophe of 1848, that Ellen Downing first made intimate acquaintance with the writings of Saint Alphonsus de Liguori, and fell under their sway.* There are several poems in this volume which show what was the intensity of her devotion to that great saint and doctor, whose name she was allowed to choose on entering religion and to which she clung when obliged, by sickness, to return to her home. His teachings were the

---

* See the poem to Saint Alphonsus, page 162. In fourth stanza, read *book* for *look*.

guide of her spiritual life; in his written prayers she found a channel for her piety; and as Saint Alphonsus, in the short intervals of his busy life, as missionary and bishop, poured out the tenderness of his soul in poetry, so did his spiritual daughter preserve in poetry the meditations and experiences of her life of suffering.

Of that life it must suffice here to say, that she became a novice in the North Presentation Convent, Cork, in October, 1849. In April, 1850, she wrote: "I like my vocation better and better, and every day I am more and more ready to confess my folly in not having sooner listened to it. You say you pray for my happiness, and there are hours in which I could say to you that your prayers are over-abundantly heard. But I would rather that you would pray for something better worth—strong virtues that would make me independent of happiness." If by happiness were meant enjoyment, her desire was granted; for she secured those strong virtues which made her find all happiness in suffering. This is expressed with too much reality in many of the following poems to be taken as the language of poetic fervour.

Father Russell tells us that, "before Miss Downing had quite completed her first year under the holy roof which she had hoped was to shelter her during the remaining days of her pilgrimage, the mysterious infirmity, which was to be her intermittent martyrdom for another score of years, declared itself in such a way that the physicians pronounced her unfit for the duties of a nun's life. It never seems to have been paralysis in the ordinary sense of the term. In the years which followed, after having been forced to be helpless and prostrate for days, and sometimes weeks, she would suddenly recover her physical energy so far as to walk about as usual. She had great power of self-control, even in very acute pain, and to the last her mind was always perfectly clear and collected. I fear we must distrust her assurance in one of her letters that she did not suffer great pain in these attacks."

That the physical sufferings here spoken of were sometimes united with the most terrible mental agony is evident from the exquisite poems called "Breathing Time," at page 84, and by that called "Darkest before Dawn," at page 109, which no one can read without compassion and admiration.

Some time after leaving the Presentation nuns she became a member of the Third Order of Saint Dominic; "and while residing in her own house, like the glorious Saint Catherine of Siena, who belonged to the same Order, or finally in a hospital, she lived faithfully to the end as a strictly observant Dominican Tertiary." For the history of her interior life, her sufferings, her good works during the last twenty years of her life, and of her most pathetic and holy death, the reader must be referred to her biographers. He will exclaim, as he lays down those records, in the words of Sister Mary Alphonsus herself:—

> "O Lord! 'tis a royal sight to see
> A soul that is truly possessed by Thee,
> Where faith is glowing in heart and brain,
> Where self is vanquished, and love doth reign."

It would be a mere impertinence to point out to the reader the spiritual beauty of the following poems, or the literary excellence of many of them. But as they are not all equally finished, it is right to state the mode of their composition. Her biographer says: "Her poems were for the most part composed when she was in the greatest suffering." This did not, however, impart to them any tinge of melancholy. She knew nothing of the melodious wailings of despair in which the modern infidel is wont to tell the world his grief. The cross produced in her strength and joy and thanksgiving. Hers were

> "the sorrows that bring
> The soul-stirring music to heart and to string."*

It would even seem that suffering was necessary to

---

* See page 118, and the beautiful poem, "Light through Darkness," at page 9 draw out her sweetest melody. Alluding to some poems, written during an interval of health, she said: "The verses are not, I think, quite worthless, but they are poor, unfilled, and merely suggest the subject. I think it is the life I lead at present which unspiritualizes me to that degree that I am incapable of writing on sacred subjects anything worthy of the name of poetry. When I am alone and in pain, when my senses are less gratified, my *outside heart* less satisfied, I shall be likely again to enter that region of the soul whose language is poetry."

Yet it must be confessed that there is sometimes perceptible a want of literary finish, and that, had strength and leisure been given her for revision, some few words would have been better selected, some redundancies cut off. A few extracts from her letters to the Bishop of Dromore, her spiritual director and superior, will not only be a full apology, should any be needed, but will give the reader a deeper interest in these compositions as the fruits not only of talent and poetic sensibility, but of prayer, and suffering, and humility.

"I have a particular affection," she writes, "for such poems as occur to me before the Blessed Sacrament." "You would be amused," she says in another letter, "at the multitude of verses which are mocking my inability to write them down. I send you the longest prayed for, though not, I think, the most successful." Later on she writes: "I am afraid sometimes that my poor verses may be teasing to you now; but it is always before the Blessed Sacrament that they occur to me, and this makes me hasten to send them to you, as if you might like them on that account."

We are deeply grateful to Dr. Leahy, the Bishop of Dromore, for cultivating and gathering these fruits of holy contemplations. Sister Mary Alphonsus had been encouraged in the work of composing by the love of souls. In the petition to St. Alphonsus, at page 88, she says:—

> "Make my writings like your own,
> Fenced by prayer still stronger;
> May their work of love go on
> When I write no longer."

"In the year 1868," writes Mother Mary Imelda, "her spiritual father and friend had more than a hundred poems printed in a little volume. She wrote to thank him in a few touching words: 'How I wish to thank you and to tell that, though not in a state for feeling, I *know* what you are doing for me in enabling me to leave behind even one little volume that will work for God after I die. This was an earnest desire until all desires died; it is again a desire, since God will have it so. Whatever name you select for the little book will be dearer to me than any I could give it. You have only hastily-written draughts of my verses; they grew more finished in my mind afterwards. Sometimes the mere alteration of a word makes a great difference. I mention this that you may let me correct the poems, if you think well; of course I have no desire to do so, if you do not wish it.' Those who have experience of authorship," continues her biographer, "will be able to appreciate the spirit of holy indifference which could make her willing to let her poems go to the world in their first hastily-written form, instead of the much more finished style in which they were then clearly before her own mind. God was pleased that she should have the full merit of the act, for sickness increased so rapidly as to render the correction of them impossible."

The present volume contains a large number of poems that were not in the former edition, but have since been collected. Perhaps some of the most touching of all her verses will be found among those now first printed. Father Russell most truly says: " Since Father Robert Southwell died a martyr, no holier tome of verse has been put into print in English or in any other language;" and he suggests that if "Voices from the Heart" was an appropriate title for the volume first printed during the life-time of the writer, "Voices from Heaven" would be a fit name for this edition. Sister Mary Alphonsus was wont to call the angels her "dear music-masters." Now that her voice is mingling with theirs before the throne of God, may she obtain the blessing which she always prayed for on earth for all the readers of these noblest of Irish Melodies.

Feast of the Purification, 1880.

CONTENTS.

	PAGE
A Prayer for the truant Gift of Song	17
To the greater Glory of God	18
Heaven	19
Mother all pure	21
To my Guardian Angel	21
Before the Blessed Sacrament	22
Light and Shade	24
Hope	25
My own Saint Alphonsus	25
Look Forward	27
The Name of Mary	28
The Angels	29
Forget me not	31
Holy Spells	32
Saint Dominic	33
Queen of the Most Sacred Rosary	35
Vocation	36
The Days when we were Happy	37
Sisters Three	38
All for God	38
Forgive me	39
Saint Agnes	40
Come back to me	41
In earnest	42
Comfort for my Angel	42
Night watching	43
Jesus and Mary	44
Twofold Martyrdom	45

	PAGE
The Cross	46
The Daisy and the Rose	47
The Prophecy of Simeon	48
Light through Darkness	49
The Minstrel's Gift	50
Devotedness	51
Saint Thomas of Aquin	52
"All to all"	56
The Poor	57
Our Elder Brothers	59
Thine and Mine	60
The Branch of green Palms and the Crown of red Roses	60
The Sun-Dial	61
My Prayer to Saint Teresa	62
The Ten Commandments	64
The Voice of the Sanctuary	65
Shadows on our Path	66
Saint Lewis and the Flowers	67
Past and Present	69
Names at Confirmation	69
Saint Joseph	71
Pure Gold for the Shrine	72
A cry in temptation	73
Angels of Strength	74
Freedom	75
The Flight into Egypt	75
The Defence in the Hall	76
When to surrender and when to hold fast	77
The Gift for the Giver	78
The Spanish Lady	79
A Word for Holy Images	82
Breathing Time	84
The Lost Talisman	85
What my Angel could do for me	86
A Petition to Saint Alphonsus	88
The Mercy of God	89
Daily Communion	91
Nature's Book	92
The Legacy	93
To the Lamp before the Blessed Sacrament	95
All for Love	96
Saints and Sinners	97

	PAGE
Spiritual Scenery	98
Hero Worship	100
My God and my All	101
May Wreaths	103
Sainted Sisters	105
Intercession of the Thrones	106
On the Death of a young Friend	107
The Stranger	108
The Sun-Flower	108
Darkest before Dawn	109
Daily Bread	111
Saint Pius V.	112
The Withered Flower	114
"Salus Infirmorum"	115
Music on the Mountain	116
Fireworks	117
The Shrine of Saint James	118
Why do we kneel to Her?	119
The Contest	120
The Communion of Saints	122
The Power of Art	123
For my dear Music-Masters	124
Cries to God	125
Hope for the Valiant	127
The Loss of the Child Jesus	128
The old Church at Lismore	128
The Sweetness of serving God	131
Fiat	131
Our best Friend	132
The Vigils of Saint Dominic	133
Choose Wisely	135
The Sacraments	135
Gold or Lead	138
Desolation	139
The Angel Guide	139
Laurels Won	140
The Royal Way of the Cross	141
Saint Alexius	142
A Cure for Sadness	144
My Holy Beads and Medals blest	145
Ballad Songs for the People	147
Angels and Birds	149

CONTENTS.

	PAGE
Feast of the Transfiguration	149
Mother of Mercy	150
The Legend of Blessed Imelda	151
A Parent's Prayer	154
The Treasure of Love	155
Dewdrops on Thorns	156
Love's Trials	157
Shifting Scenes	159
Our Holy Mother the Church	160
Aspiration	161
Remember me	161
To Saint Alphonsus on my twenty-sixth birthday	162
The Outlaw	164
Verses for every Hour in the Day	165
Light on the Hill-top	172
Mount Thabor	172
Swan-like	174
Harbour the Harbourless	174
The Angel-Keepers	175
God in All	176
To the Heart of Saint Philip Neri	176
"Taste and See"	177
The Valiant Woman	178
Everything for Thee	180
Defence	181
Taking Sanctuary	181
The Vision of Saint Agnes of Montepulciano	182
Mary and Martha	183
The Tabernacle	184
Saint Wilfrid and Rome	186
To my Creator	189
Night and Morning	189
Our Living Rosary	190
The Crucifix	191
An Act of Homage	192
Confidence	193
England	194
Mother of Christ	195
Saint Rose and her Flowers	195
Phases of Love	196
Church Flowers	198
The Answering Picture	199

CONTENTS.

	PAGE
"Thy Will be done"	200
The Curé d'Ars	202
Cross and Crown	204
Viaticum	205
Mourn for the Holy Images	206
Fetters	207
Saint Teresa watching the Blessed Sacrament	208
Solitude	210
Servants of Mary	210
Lines written in Blessed Henry Suso's "Little Book of the Eternal Wisdom"	211
The Secret of the Saints	213
To the Rebuking Angels	214
Sunshine through Showers	215
Father Louis Da Ponte	215
Comfort	217
Saint Elizabeth of Hungary	219
The Meeting	221
The Angelic Doctor	222
Festival Ground	223
Magdalen's Love	225
To Saint Raphael	226
Darkness	227
Blessed James of Mevania	227
My Three Acts	229
"Queen of Martyrs"	230
Strength before Sweetness	231
Weeds and Flowers	232
The Royal Name of Mary	233
Eternity Transmutes	234
The Welcome Visitor	235
The Prayer of Father Dominic	237
The Ways of God	238
Home Sickness	239
Assumption Morning	240
A Song of the Seasons	241
Hours of Idleness	242
Wishes	243
The Bell	243
Hope Deferred	244
The Dreams of Saint Lewis Bertrand	245
"The Lily among Thorns"	248

CONTENTS.

	PAGE
The Last Combat	248
Mother of God	250
A Hymn for October	250
Beads from the Holy Sepulchre	254
Final Perseverance	255
Homeward Bound	255
Disappointment	256
Saint Sebastian	257
My Times are in Thy Hand	258
Prayer	259
Mary is our Queen	259
White Lilies	261
The Particular Judgment	262
Extreme Unction	262
Snow Wreaths	264
A Premium for Silence	265
The Lasting Treasure	266
Our Lady of the Sacred Heart	267
Blessings	267
Solace for the Weak	269
The Wings of my Angel	270
Blessed Maria Bartholomæa	271
Work for Saint Patrick	273
Music worth waiting for	274
Home	275
The Presentation Nun	276
Charitas	278
A Legend of Melleraye	279
Night Thoughts	283
My Prayer to Saint Dominic	284
Our Constant Companions	285
Love's Yearnings	286
Meeting Saint Alphonsus in Heaven	287
Varieties	288
"Queen of all Saints"	290
Upland	291
Foreshadowing	293
Welcome Home	293
The Call of the Bridegroom	294
The New and the Old	295
The Offering	296

Voices from the Heart.

A PRAYER FOR THE TRUANT GIFT OF SONG.

GIVE me my early gift, and then
    No more for earth that gift shall be;
Make me a minstrel once again,
    That I may sing sweet songs to Thee.
My early fire is quenched, I know,
    My early faith hath fallen away;
I have no thoughts for earth, but oh!
    Fill all my soul with heaven to-day.

Now, when the wings aspire to rise,
    Why must their flight so straitened be?
Now, when the voice would reach the skies,
    Hath it no help at all from Thee?
Ah! 'tis the doom they earn too well
    Who sing of world so false as this,
That when they will, they cannot tell
    Of purer joys and higher bliss.

Well did I know the gold was Thine,
   And only given in trust to me!
Yet, laid on many an earthly shrine
   So much, there's little left for Thee:
But still, the gold that's cherished most,
   The heart which taught the songs to roam,
Was not so altogether lost,
   But Thou hast brought the wanderer home.

And though the gift be wholly fled,
   Though I can never tell in song
How much I mourn for all I said
   In praise of danger or of wrong:
A dearer joy my tears have brought—
   To lean this heart upon Thine own,
And feel that each repentant thought
   Is dearly prized and fully known.

I thank Thee, Lord! for all the pains
   That wrenched this trembling heart within;
I bless the hand that broke the chains
   Which bound me to this world of sin.
If I had songs in countless store,
   For Thee they'd charm the souls of men;
But if my silence please Thee more,
   I'll never wish to sing again.

TO THE GREATER GLORY OF GOD.

They come at Thy bidding all gushing and free,
   As streams rush along when the ice is unbound;
Their silence was only a homage to Thee,
   And now, at Thy summons, how joyful they sound;

My heart is a lute and its chords are all Thine,
   It can only make melody under Thy hand;
Far rather in silence 'twould slumber and pine,
   Than live in sweet music till Thou dost command.

Oh! cast through my spirit the seed it must sow,
   Awake every image that's pleasing to Thee;
I only can offer what Thou dost bestow,
   I only can whisper what's whispered to me.
Oh! take from Thy minstrel all life of her own,
   May Thy praise and Thy pleasure her happiness be;
And though all the laurels of earth were her own,
   Be it still her sweet triumph to yield them to Thee.

HEAVEN.

Lift up thine eyes and see,
   With rapture past the telling,
What God hath stored for thee
   In His eternal dwelling:
The joys that ne'er are o'er,
   The wreaths no blight can wither
Are thine for evermore,
   When death will send thee thither.

Unnumbered angels greet
   The soul that bursts her prison,
And sing their anthems sweet
   Around the newly risen;
While she takes up the lay
   With joy no words can measure,
And fast begins her day
   Of never-ending pleasure.

O Love! what must it be
   To soar on fearless pinion,
Where all is filled with Thee
   And under Thy dominion!
To scale so grand a height,
   To see as Thou art seeing,
And drink in new delight
   With every tide of being!

To kneel at Mary's feet
   And bless the hand that crowned her,
To mark the anthems sweet
   That swell and float around her;
And, through the wondrous rays
   Of deepening light above her,
To meet at last the gaze
   Of our eternal Lover!

To hail those founts of love,
   Those piteous wounds so gory—
No bleeding wounds above
   But streams of life and glory:—
To hear Him bless the day
   In which His Heart's-blood won us,
And feel the warming ray
   Of His sweet eyes upon us!

O God! how rich my gain,
   How cheaply won my treasure,
E'en with a life of pain
   To buy an endless pleasure.
Oh, grant me grace to bless
   The cross which Thou hast given,
Until my lips shall press
   Thine own dear wounds in heaven.

MOTHER ALL PURE.

All pure—without a single spot
   To stain thy soul at all,
Alone its beauty altered not
   At the primeval fall:
In every other God could see
   Some blemish not to love,
But never found a spot in thee,
   His "Perfect One," His "Dove."

The mirror of thy virgin mind,
   Unbreathed upon and bright,
Gives back the Godhead there enshrined
   In full, eternal light:
The purest angel dimly knows,
   What wealth of joy is thine
Whose heart still opens, like the rose,
   To light and warmth divine.

The Child upon thy bosom pressed
   Or in thine arms entwined,
Best knew the secrets of the breast
   To which He was consigned:
And ever from His God-like hand
   Such glory shower'd on thee
As men can never understand,
   But well might die to see.

TO MY GUARDIAN ANGEL.

O gentle Angel! ask for me
   From Mary, Queen above,
A snow-white robe of purity,
   A golden crown of love:

Remind her of the pledge I gave
  To love but only One,
And say that every gift I crave
  Will deck me for her Son.

O faithful Angel! think how soon
  The fleeting breath must part,
And kindly win one Godlike boon
  For this poor stricken heart.
Too little hath it lived for love,
  It fain for love would die;
Then ask one dart from heaven above
  To pierce it for the sky.

O glorious Angel! when the light
  Of life these eyes shall see,
And the quick torrents of delight
  Rush down from God to me:
With love that earth hath never known,
  With burst of song and prayer,
I'll bless, before the eternal throne,
  My Guardian Angel's care.

BEFORE THE BLESSED SACRAMENT.

Kindest friends can never be
  Like to you, great God of love,
  Who, from heaven's bright home above,
Still watch on earth with me.
Human ties are false and weak,
  Breaking heart they seldom cheer;
But no aching heart can seek
  Anything it finds not here,
              Dear God!

Oh, that lamp which burns so bright,
   Telling that my God is nigh!
   Never sunbeam from the sky
Cheered me like that lonely light.
Why am *I* alone before you?
   Have not all men equal claim?—
True, the angels here adore You,
   But 'twas not for *them* you came,
                Dear God!

Wretched world! too much deceiving
   Hearts for which my Saviour died,
   Still your pleasure and your pride
Were the source of all His grieving.
Ever more you lure away
   Souls that shrink and hearts that falter;
O that they would list and pray
   Where He speaks from yonder altar,
                Dear God!

Am I not too happy here,
   Everything I want imploring,
   All my soul bowed down adoring,
Loving till I cannot fear?
Wherefore come you thus to me—
   God beside me—God above?
There you're throned in majesty,
   Here you're lost in love,
                Dear God!

Oh, may labour, pain, and prayer
   Help me to repay this loving,
   All my grateful fondness proving
With a life's untiring care.

Let not such a mighty wonder
    Fail its work to do;
Break at last the bonds asunder
    Keeping back from you
                Great God!

LIGHT AND SHADE.

"Benedicite lux et tenebræ Domino."—Dan. iii. 72.

Oh! now my heart is alive with joy
    And then it is dead with woe,
Now, glad in the light of the summer warmth,
    Then, chilled by the frost and snow;
But as every old year dies away,
    And every new comes forth,
I'm taking it less and less to heart
    If I suffer or smile on earth.

I know the pains in themselves are best,
    But never can dare to say,
When pleasure looks forth with her smiling face,
    "I'd rather have pain to-day:"
For if sorrow should come at the Master's call,
    The Master would bear me through,
But how do I know, if I sent for it,
    What mischievous things 'twould do?

For ever the angels are teaching me,
    The wisdom of man doth lie
In taking the day as it comes to him
    And working while life goes by;
In taking the day as it comes to him
    And using the tools at hand,
And asking the tears and the smiles alike
    To bring him to Fatherland.

HOPE.

Prayers won't be always vain,
Thought won't be always pain,
Bright days will come again
                For you and me.

Sad sighs will all be o'er,
Salt tears will fall no more,
Then shall we sing and soar,
                Happy and free.

Blessing the God that gave
Courage and hope to brave
Rude wind and stormy wave,
                On life's dark sea.

MY OWN ST. ALPHONSUS.

Looking to the saints above
   All is bliss and glory,
Thinking of the saints below,
   'Tis another story.
Oh, my dear and sainted guide!
   Now high-throned in heaven,
How, by many a rending pang,
   Thy great heart was riven!

Partings that dashed out thy youth
   With its dream of pleasure,
Secret groans when all were gone,
   Tears that knew no measure;

Scorn still crossed thy noblest aims,
    Slander's dart o'ertook thee;
Lights of earth so rudely quenched,
    God's own light forsook thee.

Wasting sickness, oh! how long,
    Mocked thy free endeavour,
And, in parting, left behind
    Its sharp sting for ever:
Evil tongues and hellish plots
    Spread such snares about thee,
They who would have loved thee most
    Seemed compelled to doubt thee.

Oh, my dear and weeping saint!
    All His anguish sharing—
Like thy Master's, was the crown
    Thou didst die in wearing:
There where surest faith should lie,
    Fraud and wrong beset thee;
There where help seemed bound to be,
    Oh! what falsehood met thee.

Thinking on thy life, it seems
    Mine must change or lose thee;
I would blush to shrink from pain,
    Yet for name-saint choose thee:
I will take the pain, and then
    I may call thee "Father;"
I will only ask through life
    Wreaths like thine to gather.

LOOK FORWARD.

Life is not too long for sorrow,
Death will make a brighter morrow;
They that here have hardest striven
Take the sweetest rest in heaven.

Every moment spent for pleasure
Steals from an eternal treasure;
Every battle lost or won
Earns a judgment or a crown.

None have made too swift beginning,
Time was never lent for sinning;
Senseless! what do you delay for,
Wasting hours that God would pay for?

Strive the more and speed the faster,
Hired by such a mighty Master:
Sinless maid and martyr hoary
Cheaply win their cloudless glory.

Ah! be wise—let all be given,
Purchase all you can from heaven;
Here you'll leave whate'er you love—
Purchase sure estates above.

Sell you every moment high—
Let not paltry bidders buy:
God demanding, ne'er withhold;
God can always pay in gold.

Learn the proper use of pain,—
Tears should never flow in vain;
All the dead have wept and striven,
All have not been crown'd in heaven.

Trust no phantom-future splendid;
Life will cease when strife is ended;
Once the foe is dead or taken,
Battlefields are soon forsaken.

Life is not too long for sorrow,
Death will make a brighter morrow;
Here we'll fight, and if victorious,
There we'll reign all crown'd and glorious.

THE NAME OF MARY.

The peaceful name of Mary!
  When day is at its close,
And weary hearts and eyelids
  Are yearning for repose;
Sleep falls in dreams more holy,
  Rest shows her form more fair,
Where the sweet name of Mary
  Hath closed the evening prayer.

The blessed name of Mary!
  When morn is up once more,
And hearts new-born from slumber
  Are hastening to adore:
Still morning joy grows deeper,
  As wakes on every tongue
The joyful name of Mary,
  From whom our JOY hath sprung.

The royal name of Mary!
  When storms are raging round,
And many a fierce temptation
  Would hurl us to the ground;
'Tis then, in grief and danger,
  We turn our Queen to view,
And the great name of Mary
  Still bears us bravely through.

The heaven-taught name of Mary!
  When death itself draws near,
And the poor heart is aching
  With many an anxious fear;
This name, which blessed our childhood,
  And check'd youth's headlong course,—
The conquering name of Mary,
  Then most we'll prove its force.

THE ANGELS.

I'm alone, and yet I am not alone,
  For the Angels are always near me,
And I never can pray in so faint a tone
  But the watchful Angels hear me:
I know they are twining a choral lay
  To the throne of God up springing,
So I hush my heart for the live-long day
  In hopes I may hear them singing.

I'm told there are Angels as far—as far
  As a human thought can wander,
And I think there's an Angel to every star,
  To teach us to look beyond her;

For, oh! while I gazed on the heavens last night,
  I read on their face a story
Which caught up my breast from the silvery light
  To Him who awoke its glory.

There are Angels so near to the throne of God
  They seem but the gems beneath it,
There are Angels to smile on the humblest sod
  Where the prayer of a child has breathèd;
There are Angels to watch by the graves we love,
  And when we are kneeling near them,
They speak to our hearts of a God above
  Who knows His own time to cheer them.

The Angels are with us by night and by day,
  Our faith and our hope renewing;
They nerve when we labour, they bless when we pray,
  They love us whatever we're doing.
Oh, sweet is the love of an Angel's heart;
  It never knows change nor tiring;
Though from every friend upon earth you part—
  Be true to its deep inspiring.

There's an Angel to hallow the poor man's birth,
  And to welcome the homeless stranger,
And—blessed be God who so loves the earth—
  There's an Angel to every danger.
Our lives are so circled by Angel bands
  They brighten the way before us,
And we never can sail to such far-off lands
  But *they* will be watching o'er us.

The poor are the same as the rich to them—
  Or if not the same—'tis only
That sometimes the Angels feel more for them
  They are so unloved and lonely.

Oh, true is the guard which the Angels keep!
  Oh, long may they watch anigh us!
If ever we dream of our God in sleep,
  'Tis because there's an Angel by us.

Then glory to God for the Angels' powers,
  And thanks for the charge He gave them,
To shine on these wandering hearts of ours,
  To succour, and shield, and save them.
Still, still may we tread in the Angels' track,
  Still trust to the Angels' showing,
That so, when He calleth our Angels back,
  We too may be fit for going.

"FORGET ME NOT."

O LORD! I am a wretched worm,
  Unworthy Thine and Thee;
The smallest favour from Thy hand
  Is far too good for me;
For I was nothing ere my birth,
  And well may hide my brow,
Because I am but sinful earth,
  More vile than nothing now.

But, Lord, 'twas time to think of this
  Ere Thou hadst left Thy throne,
To seek a dwelling in my heart,
  And win it for Thine own.

Now, made Thy temple and Thy spouse,
  It well befits Thy care,
And still "the beauty of Thy house"
  Shall animate my prayer.

HOLY SPELLS.

Long ago I feared to use
"Holy spells," lest they should lose,
By a touch so little pure,
All their power to bless and cure.

I was bold enough to say,
I could take the charm away,
Which Christ's holy Church had set
On her prayer-touched amulet.

Now I know, for sinner's need
Come the Medal and the Bead,
And that contrite sinner's touch
Ne'er can seek them overmuch.

Now I wear them all the day,
Lift them boldly when I pray,
Clasp at night with fonder care,
Thinking of their ceaseless prayer.

Souls, you little know your loss
In the Medal and the Cross,
And the fond alluring Bead,
Tempting one to intercede.

SAINT DOMINIC.

The legends of Saint Dominic
   Have traced him firm and true,
As one who ceased not in his prayer,
   Yet worked the whole day through;
Of dauntless mind to think and plan,
   To labour and to dare,
With heart to pour its fulness out
   In mercy and in prayer.
By night he bared his soul to God,
   By day he worked for men;
Oh, how the world would stand amazed
   If Dominic lived again!

'Tis told of our Saint Dominic
   How, when his course began,
A preacher to a faithless race—
   A marked and hunted man—
Though snares were on his daily path
   He never turned aside,
But trusted in the God above
   To guard him and to guide:
And wherefore should he faint or fear,
   Whose death would be his gain,
And all whose treasure seemed to lie
   In poverty and pain?

  Our blessed Father Dominic
   So loved the house of God,
'Twas there he took his chosen rest
   Whatever land he trod;

And though the gates had all been shut,
    He still went in to pray,
Because an angel smote the bars
    Which stopped him on his way:
So thus he kept his nightly watch,
    And when the daylight rose
Went forth to bless the friends of God,
    And triumph o'er His foes.

The great and glorious Dominic
    Had fixed his hopes above;
His wealth was all in suffering,
    His life was all in love:
He little cared to have or hoard,
    But sometimes begged his way,
And sometimes asked an alms from heaven,
    As he knelt down to pray;
Whene'er his brethren fail'd or feared,
    Or found the road too long,
He paused to rest their weariness,
    But else he journeyed on.

The faith of great Saint Dominic
    Was never seen to dim;
Once man begins to work for God,
    'Tis God that works by him.
He touched the sick with healing power,
    He stilled the words of strife,
He led the wanderer back to heaven,
    He raised the dead to life.
When threat'ning torrents crossed his path
    He meekly blessed and trod,
For not a wave had power against
    His childlike faith in God.

And this was our Saint Dominic
   Who left a type so true,
In mantle black and tunic white,
   Of what his own should do:
And if he loved his children well
   While yet on earth he trod,
And fondly watched o'er every soul
   Which he had won for God,
Much more his love from heaven above
   Will look, with kindliest care,
On him who treads in Dominic's steps,
   And trusts in Dominic's prayer.

QUEEN OF THE MOST SACRED ROSARY.

O JOYFUL Heart of Mary!
   What trembling bliss was thine,
Thy Son and God to worship
   Within His humble shrine!
To watch His infant footsteps,
   To guard His infant rest,
Within thine arms to shield Him,
   And clasp Him to thy breast.

O mournful Heart of Mary!
   To meet that cruel day,
When rent, and racked, and tortured,
   Upon the cross He lay;
To feel His bitter anguish,
   To hear His dying cry,
To see His death-thirst mocked at,
   And then to see Him die!

O glorious Heart of Mary!
  O wonder-spot above!
Where God hath all surpassed Himself
  In royalty and love:
For every pang a glory,
  For every prayer a wreath,—
His crowning grace above thee,
  His brightest saints beneath!

But, sweet and joyful Mother,
  Mother of tears and woe,
Mother of grace and glory,
  Thou still hast cares below!
Then bid us share thy rapture,
  And bid us taste thy pain,
To sing at last thy grandeur
  In Christ's eternal reign.

VOCATION.

Full often I am thinking
  Of a bard who used to go
Beside the field of battle,
  Where he never struck a blow;
For though sick and lame and feeble,
  He was useless in the field,
Still he nerved its heroes onwards
  With the music he could yield.

Thus I fain would sing of battles
  That I never come to share,
Would tempt the wings of others
  To the flight I cannot dare;

And since in God's high combat
   Lance or sword I may not wield,
Give Him music from my heartstrings
   For his heroes in the field.

THE DAYS WHEN WE WERE HAPPY.

Do you think we would be happy
   If the cross should come no more,
Flinging shadows on the green sward
   As it used to do before?
Do you think we would be happy
   If the pains were gone to rest,
Which have found us at His table,
   And have laid us on His breast?

Do you think we would be happy
   If a carpet way was spread
Where the confessors have sorrowed,
   And the faithful martyrs bled?
Do you think we would be happy
   In our shelter near the cross,
To think *we* had all the glory
   And that *He* had all the loss?

Ah, no! our hearts would sicken,
   Every dawn and every day,
We'd be lonesome for the shadow
   In the fulness of the ray;
We would miss the hallowed traces
   On the footway of our God,
Till we asked some genial sorrow,
   Just to show us where He trod.

And though we may be happy
  In the absence of the ray,
With the cross for our companion,—
  The dear cross on which He lay;
If the cross itself forsake us
  With the shadow which it cast,
Our happy days for ever
  Must be counted with the past.

SISTERS THREE.

O LORD! of all the rest bereft,
Three treasures to my life are left-
Fair Poetry with Pain and Prayer
Seem truly to have settled there.

Without the last I could not thrive,
The second keeps the last alive;
The first to go or stay is free,
Yet cling they not like Sisters Three?

Their union is both close and strong,
For Pain is always prompting Song,
And Song herself would never care
To breathe, except in aid of Prayer.

ALL FOR GOD.

GIVE all to God. Remember yet
  That God gave all to you;
Whate'er you are or have, the debt
  To Him 's justly due.

The home that nursed, the love that warm'd,
   Blue sky and fragrant sod,
Whate'er has blessed or thrilled or charm'd
   Are all but gifts of God.

Give all for God. He is the spring
   Of all you most admire,
The source of every glorious thing
   That human hearts desire.

The hope for which you've learned to live,
   The friends for whom you pray,
If God should ask, oh, gladly give,
   And trust Him to repay.

FORGIVE ME.

My erring nature leads astray
   Whatever pains I take,
I always seek the perfect way,
   And evermore mistake:
So much of evil enters there,
   Whatever good I do—
"Forgive me" seems the only prayer
   That I can make to You.

"Forgive me," then; in this is *all*,
   'Tis here my safety lies;
Forgive my rashness when I fall,
   My weakness when I rise.

Thy mercy sheds the only ray
    That lights my soul to heaven;
I cannot think, nor act, nor pray,
    Except to be *forgiven*.

SAINT AGNES.

Her cheek was not a shade more pale,
    She wore no look of pride;
She gently drew the amber veil
    Of her long hair aside.

No stern defiance taught her eye
    To smile upon the glaive,
She simply felt it sweet to die
    And meant not to be brave.

She scarcely seemed the angry eyes
    Of her stern judge to see,
She scarcely heard the muttered cries
    Reversing his decree.

She scarcely felt the lightning stroke
    Which hurled her on the sod;
'Twas a short dream from which she woke
    To her embracing God.

Her love had been a virgin love,
    Her brow a virgin brow;
And virgins twine her wreath above,
    And seek her shrine below.

Death found her in her bridal dress,
   And heard her bridal vows;
She passed in bridal tenderness
   To her eternal Spouse.

COME BACK TO ME.

My God! my Love! come back to me,
My soul hath bitter need of Thee;
I cannot love, I cannot pray,
I cannot rest me night or day
In quiet thoughts of heaven and Thee:
My God! my Love! come back to me.

Mysterious God! so far, so near,
Faith only tells me Thou art here;
As ever on thy bounty fed,
As ever by Thy wisdom led,
Thy gifts have lost the look of Thee:
My God! my Love! come back to me.

Thou knowest 'tis but Thyself alone
Can fill the heart Thyself hast won;
If Thou shouldst give me leave to go
Back to the world, I could not now.
Poor and alone! I cry to Thee:
My God! my Love! come back to me.

IN EARNEST.

"In earnest" is a word of power,
  It strives with sin and woe,
It fights its battles every hour,
  And conquers every foe;
It takes the road it meant at first,
  It keeps it night and day;
The beam may warm, the cloud may burst,
  It turns not from its way.

The earnest soul will capture heaven,
  Whate'er her state may be;
The strongest chains can still be riven
  By them that would be free.
Pray, with a firm resolve to *do*,
  And God will aid the right,
But crowns were never meant for you
  Who never dare to fight.

COMFORT FOR MY ANGEL.

How hard it seems for thee, Angel bright,
  With thy beautiful wings and free,
To shut thyself up all day, all night,
  In a lonely room with me.

I know thy heaven is the will divine,
  That the face of thy God is here,
That thy life has nothing alike to mine,
  Though our being is bound so near.

But however I know it, to think and say,
   At times I forget it all;
And I pity my Angel held fast all day.
   In such dark and weary thrall.

'Tis then that I do for thee, Angel bright,
   What oft thou hast done for me,
Still striving to speak, in my pain's despite,
   Some comforting words to thee.

I talk of the day that will call thee back
   To thy smiling heaven once more,
And how thou wilt bear on the refound track
   A companion to its fair shore.

I shorten the days that appear so long
   By telling thee how they fly,
And that one or another in speeding on
   Will certainly see me die;

That then, in that moment of bliss for each,
   The meaning of pain thou'lt see,
And regret shall never thy kind heart reach
   For what it endured for me.

NIGHT WATCHING.

The shepherds watch the midnight skies,
   The star appears in view;
Such star to every soul will rise
   That keeps the night-watch true.

The trembling Shepherds faint for fear,
    The Angels calm their dread;
An Angel's voice each one shall hear
    That humbly bows the head.

The adoring Shepherds rise with speed
    And quick the word fulfil;
Oh! follow as the Shepherds lead,
    And we shall find Him still.

JESUS AND MARY.

WHERE shall an Infant God be sought
    But at a Virgin's breast?
Can we adore the Son, and not
    Believe the Mother blest?
Where shall we fondly hail the bud
    But on the parent stem?
How can we look to Jesus' blood
    And Mary's tears contemn?

Seek we the Mother with the Son,
    The Son beside the Mother,
For vainly would we bless the One
    If we should slight the other:
So linked in labours, love, and pain,
    Her heart for His so riven,
Mary will never plead in vain
    While Jesus rules in heaven.

TWOFOLD MARTYRDOM.

Saint Sebastian was condemned by the Emperor Dioclesian to be shot to death with arrows. His acts relate that, recovering by the care of the pious Lady Irene, he suffered a second and glorious martyrdom at Rome, A. D. 288.

THROUGH all that weary martyrdom, my own beloved Saint!
Thy high hope bore thee up to heaven, thy spirit did not faint;
The weariness, the loneliness, the sharp, protracted pain,
Were but, to thy heroic soul, a glory and a gain.

The straining of thy tortured limbs, the dimness of thine eyes,
The fainting of thy worn-out frame like death upon thee lies;
But when the careless marksmen shout that now their work is done,
Oh! truest martyr that thou art, *thy* crown has not been won.

Oh! what a waking from the tomb—on earth, on earth once more,
The battle to be fought anew, so bravely won before,
The distant heaven receding far, that seemed so close that day,
With pain and chill uncertainty again upon thy way.

But wast thou not a martyr more, returning from the grave
Than when the pointed arrows all their sharpest torments gave?

And was not such rekindling life an arrow meant
  to be
More potent executioner of God's high will on thee?

Oh! meekly didst thou bow thy head while waiting
  for the crown,
And calmly didst thou cast thy hope at God's high
  mandate down;
And sweetly didst thou meet thy life, to bear its load
  anew,
All thou hadst done, and more than all, content
  again to do.

High Saint! if I have knelt before to claim a thought
  from thee,
Because such pangs as pierced thy flesh in my heart
  seemed to be,
I here can press a stronger claim, so oft recalled to
  life,
When heaven had all but promised me the closing
  of the strife.

THE CROSS.

How helplessly I seem to cling
  About thy Cross to-day,
As if it should supply to me
  For all it takes away;
And, though it is so rude a bed,
  I know it still to be
The very safest resting-place
  In all the world for me.

Was I not fostered in its arms
  And fed upon its fruit?
And in its month of early flowers
  Did I not see them shoot?
And did I not its fragrance smell,
  And taste its honey too,
And won't I now have faith in it
  For all it means to do?

'Tis not because my heart sends forth
  A sudden shriek, whene'er
Its iron arm hath work to do
  Which flesh and blood must fear,
That after just a moment's thought
  I cannot turn and say,
Dear Cross, kind Cross, do all thy work,
  And do it thy own way.

Oh! let us see the joys depart,
  They only came to go
When they had girded for the fight,
  And strengthened for the woe;
They only came as heralds sure
  Of brighter joys to be,
When the dear Cross has done its work,
  And set the spirit free.

THE DAISY AND THE ROSE.

The Rose is queen on beauty's throne,
  Yet, if the Rose should see
No other beauty but her own,
  How lonely she would be!

Her joy is in the blessed sun
  Who makes her heart so bright,
And every flower he smiles upon
  Increases her delight.

In myriads springing at our feet,
  The humble Daisy blows,
And yet, the Daisy's life is sweet
  As any flower's that grows;
She lifts her eye at peep of day
  To see the sun come out,
And gladly welcomes every ray
  Which brightens things about.

If in this spirit I could share
  Of freedom and repose,
'Twould little matter which I were,
  A Daisy or a Rose:
Alike I'd bless the gifts of God,
  Another's or my own,
At rest upon the meanest sod
  Which looked unto His throne.

THE PROPHECY OF SIMEON.

It is a joyful mystery,
  Oh, Mother dear! for me,
Thy gentle Son in sacrifice
  Presented thus by thee;
But still my heart is far more wont
  To weep upon the doom
Which met thee at the temple gate,
  To haunt thee to His tomb.

How many a happy mother came
   And offered up her son,
Redeeming him with bird or lamb,
   And then her work was done;
But thy unequalled tenderness
   Did feel, as none can say,
The anguish of the sacrifice
   Begun upon that day.

And when thine arms received again
   Thy God to their embrace,
How mingled was thy happiness
   In looking on His face!
As still the day rose up, on which
   No dove could buy Him back,
But thy mild eyes should weep above
   The blood-marks on His track.

O Mary! turn those eyes on us
   That none have cause to flee.
Our hearts, alas! can measure not
   The debt they owe to thee:
What hymns shall e'er be vowed to thee,
   What earthly homage done
Can pay thy life-long wail above
   The death-pangs of thy Son?

LIGHT THROUGH DARKNESS.

Like lightning through a thunder cloud
   My songs leap forth to-day,
And leave my spirit in its shroud
   Of gloomy thoughts to stay;

Whatever ray hath warmed my words,
  My heart in ice is bound,
And all at war its inmost chords,
  However sweet they sound.

Yet, give my lips the blessed power
  To chant thy name, O Lord!
E'en though I feel not in that hour
  By my own music stirred:
Breathe all Thy sweetness through my lays,
  Howe'er my soul repine;
And may I sweetly sing thy praise
  For purer hearts than mine.

THE MINSTREL'S GIFT.

The women of Jerusalem,
  With homage swift and free,
Brought all their golden ornaments
  To melt them down for Thee;
Content before Thy creatures' eyes
  Less royally to shine,
For that which won a fonder glance
  From those dear eyes of Thine.

I have no golden ornaments,
  Nor do I come to lay,
Like Magdalen, a perfume rare
  Before Thy shrine to-day;
The only wealth I ever had
  In my wild harp was found,
The sweetest joys I ever knew
  Came mingling with its sound.

But I have wreathed my harp with flowers
    Of many a varied hue,—
With lily, rose, and violet,
    And love-lies-bleeding too;
And I have learned an air of love,
    And tried it o'er and o'er;
And I have brought Thee heart and harp—
    To claim them back no more.

Then wilt Thou not accept the gift
    Of heart and harp to-day,
With all the wreaths of woven flowers,
    And fond accustomed lay?
And wilt Thou not instruct the chords
    Henceforth Thine own to be,
In every sweetest art that can
    Improve their tone for Thee?

DEVOTEDNESS.

"Eat, O friends, and drink, and be inebriated, my dearly beloved."—
Cant. v. i.

O LORD! 'tis a royal sight to see
A soul that is truly possessed by Thee,
Where faith is glowing in heart and brain,
Where self is vanquished, and love doth reign

That soul shall tranquilly glide along,
Singing triumphant a swan-like song,
For her dying life, as it onward floats,
Is set to the music of angel notes.

The incense breath of the flowers shall rise,
The lavish summer expand her sighs,
And crowns and flowers profusely fall
At the feet of her who has left them all.

The soul who centres her hopes in Thee
Shall tread life's mazes with footsteps free,
While the homage that creatures around her fling
She yields in her spirit to God, their King.

Thy love hath fenced her so closely in,
No strange affection can pass within,
But whatever love she doth hear or see
Is always feeding her love for Thee.

Oh! show to the souls Thou dost love the best
The way to rise, and the place to rest:
What hope for thy Church would a phalanx be
Of queenly spirits in love with Thee!

SAINT THOMAS OF AQUIN.

Come, read about the pious child
    Who heard and kept so well
The saintly words and counsels mild
    Which from the old monks fell:
His pastime still a quiet walk,
    A legend simply told,
Or dearer yet, the holy talk
    Of Benedictines old.

Come, see how sweet the mother smiled
   To claim her child once more,
A simple, meek, and sinless child,
   Yet graver than before;
No changeling thing of smiles and tears,
   Light laugh and buoyant tone,
But wise beyond his father's years,
   And sweet beyond his own.

Come, linger by the fair domain
   Through which young Thomas moved,
The home ties at his heart again,
   All loving, all beloved;
No priestly counsels met him there,
   But wheresoe'er he trod,
His cloister was the ceaseless prayer
   His soul sent up to God.

The boy has left his home once more,
   'Mid youth and bearded men
He learns the rich and varied lore
   The world had time for then;
But well may God and angels smile,
   For tasks are nobly done
When earth is only wooed awhile,
   That heaven may yet be won.

No monks of Benedictine rule
   Are round our saint to-day,
Not through the early convent-school
   His future pathway lay:
No line of saints shall Thomas claim
   As brethren crown'd above,
But he himself a leading name
   For after-times to love.

Will a proud father scorn to see
   The path thus humbly trod?
Will a fond mother mourn to be
   Left desolate for God?
Will his warm youth be strong to meet
   A struggle fierce as this?—
Ah! he has prayed at Jesus' feet
   That God's strength might be his.

In prison-tower, the novice keeps
   His vigil long and dim;
The brothers storm, the mother weeps,
   The angels watch with him;
His sisters long have ceased to pray,
   With pleading look and tone,
For, oh! he charmed their hearts away
   To dwell beside his own.

And there, within that silent tower,
   Derided or forgot,
He sowed the seeds of future power,
   E'en while he knew it not;
For some worn volumes, scant and few,
   Conned o'er and o'er again,
Shaped forth for him the doctrine true
   Which burst like light on men.

What, if the temptress sought him there,
   Since God defends the right,
And he that never fails in prayer
   Will never fail in fight:

But ere he reaped his rich reward,
    He well and bravely strove;
Then angels bound him with the cord
    Of pure, angelic love.

The prison-tower hath loosed its hold,
    The convent smiles once more,
The habit with its sacred fold
    Is round him as before:
The brethren, and the quiet cell,
    The silent hour of prayer,
The holy choir—oh! who shall tell
    What raptures wait him there!

Grace, with its sweet, subduing power,
    Light, with its force divine,
Love, with its rich and teeming dower,
    Meet at the Saviour's shrine:
There shall the sinful weep forgiven,
    There may the weary rest,
There will the heart that hopes in heaven
    Drink of its fountains blest.

Through the still night he hears the voice
    Of Jesus break his prayer,
Making his inmost soul rejoice
    With the strong rapture there:—
"Thomas, of Me well hast thou written,
    What shall thy work reward?"
Swift was the answer, fondly given—
    "Nought but Thyself, O Lord!"

* * * * * * *
Now rest we here, for he is dying,
    The sage whom Jesus taught;
Long hath his soul for God been sighing,
    That God so early sought.
Sweetly he waits his parting hour,
    Calmly he looks above,
Still are his words the words of power,
    Still is he taught by love.

Show me a nobler life than this,
    A heart more grand and true,
Cast like a seed of future bliss,
    And ripening as it grew:
In heaven, where joys around him flow,
    May great Saint Thomas pray
For hearts still wavering here below
    That lean on his to-day.

"ALL TO ALL."

Seraph-songs delight each other,
    Happy saints sit side by side,
Good is still increased by sharing,—
    Trample down thine idiot pride:
God is all alone in glory,
    Still His works in concert shine;
Does He share thy gift with others,
    'Tis to make it doubly thine.

Scanty is thy share of being
   Who within thyself art bound;
Break from out thy wretched prison,
   Dare to dwell in palace-ground:
Love not so the life within thee,
   Losing sight of aught beside;
Thou wast made to live in all things
   Which thy God hath glorified.

Think what words will sound hereafter,—
   "Enter into joy divine,"—
What is this but love creative,
   Losing sight of *thine* and *mine*.
Love the light where'er it shineth,
   Joy the more, the more there be;
Till thy soul be fit for heaven,
   Heaven can ne'er be fit for thee.

THE POOR.

How much Christ loves the poor!
   How much He longs to be
The comfort and the cure
   Of all their misery!

He knows their piteous case,
   Unfriended and alone,
Cold, hunger, and disgrace,
   They all have been His own.

How much He longs to share
  His higher world of bliss,
With them who have to bear
  His heavy cross in this!

How pleased He is to see
  The poor about His throne!
Though friendless they may be,
  His welcome is their own.

Not any fragrant flower,
  Nor any shining gem,
With Him has so much power
  As one salt tear from them.

When incense breathes about,
  And all is grand and fair,
He still is looking out
  For his poor children there;

And when He sees them smile,
  Forgetting their own woe,
And happy for a while
  That He is honoured so,

His heart doth overflow
  In promise full and sure,
That they shall one day know
  The good of being poor.

OUR ELDER BROTHERS.

O Brethren! think on the Angels kind,
   So ready for service true,
Still plying the work with an equal mind
   Which *we* have no time to do.

They through the alleys and lanes are met,
   Waiting on maimed and poor,
Soothing the sorrows that we forget,
   The ailments that we should cure.

They round the steps of the children glide,
   Helping their souls to live,
Striving to turn their thoughts aside
   From the lessons the sinful give.

They, where the lamp of the altar shines,
   Worship both day and night,
Thanking the Lord for His sweet designs
   On hearts that neglect them quite.

They, to the prison *our* prayers should ope,
   On the pinions of love make way,
Cheering their charge with a dawning hope
   Of a ransom that we delay.

They on Christ's Mother and ours attend,
   True to her every call,
Ready their wonderful gifts to spend,
   To answer her will in all.

For, whether in zeal for the human race,
   Or in love for their God—we find,
The Angels are still in the foremost place,
   And we—oh! so far behind.

THINE AND MINE.

I CLASP Thy gifts for love of Thee,
Twice Thine, since they belong to me;
For couldst Thou lose Thy right divine,
Thou still wert Lord of me and mine.

I hold my jewels at Thy will;
Reclaimed, they are my jewels still,
Nor ever live so much for me,
As when they give themselves to Thee.

I would not rob Thee, if I could,
Of any joy or any good;
Wert Thou the poorer for my gain,
My joys would be my saddest pain.

But where I am so wholly Thine,
Thou canst not lose by what is mine;
And while Thou art so close to me,
I do not part what goes to Thee.

THE BRANCH OF GREEN PALMS AND THE CROWN OF RED ROSES.

A BRANCH of green palms and a crown of red roses,
  A gem full of lustre is SORROW to me,
Each hour that she stays some new magic discloses,
  Her chains are mysterious, and bind to set free.

In darkness she comes, but departs in such splendour
    As leaves me to sigh for her coming once more;
And though rudely she grasps, yet I dare not offend her,
    By shrinking from hands which have healed me before.

Her voice still affrights, though I hear it so often,
    But when in the silence I think what she said,
The love-laden words so my spirit can soften,
    I long for the accents which fill me with dread.

The branch of green palms and the crown of red roses,
    The gem full of lustre no more will I flee;
The word of a God her true value discloses,
    The blood of a Saviour has bought her for me.

THE SUN-DIAL.

The dial works beneath the sun
    And idles in the shower,
She is no use to anyone
    Except in smiling hour:
Yet do not chide the dial's gaze
    For waiting on the ray,
She cannot help her moping ways
    When sunshine will not play.

She was not formed to tell her tale
    Except in sunny hour,
She has no pleasure in the gale,
    No business with the shower:
She does the work with all her heart
    That she was sent to do,
Nor ever wearies of her part,
    The live-long summer through.

She has no joy but in the ray,
    Yet, never does she take
Offence to see it turn away,
    But watches for its sake:
And, when one thinks of all the days
    Her constancy has trial,
It must be owned, that she displays
    No little self-denial.

MY PRAYER TO SAINT TERESA.

O Mother, Saint Teresa,
    'Twas in mistake, one day
I called you by so fond a name;
    But ever since I pray
As if I had indeed a right
    To your especial care,
And often does your heart appear
    To open to my prayer.

O Mother, Saint Teresa,
    The books you left below
Have caused within this feeble heart
    A bold demand to grow;

Until you show what "wildfire" is,
   No pain there seems to be
From which I'd shrink, if it could light
   This mighty spark in me.

O Mother, Saint Teresa,
   How often through the day
"Love"—"wildfire" are the only words
   In which I seem to pray:
For watch and ward I'd nerve my soul,
   From ease and pleasure flee,
If I could thus induce my God
   To light this spark in me.

O Mother, Saint Teresa,
   My name-saint long ago
Was your true client,[*] till through his
   Your spirit seemed to glow;
And I can say for my own Saint,
   How much his wish would be,
That you would give him help to light
   This mighty spark in me.

O Mother, Saint Teresa,
   I'd listen night and day
To every word that leaves your lips,
   And struggle to obey;
I'd tell you all my heart and soul,
   And wait on patient knee,
If you would ask my God to light
   This blessed spark in me.

---

[*] St. Alphonsus had a most special devotion to St. Teresa.

THE TEN COMMANDMENTS.

I AM the Lord, thy God,—to claim
  Thy sovereign worship solely.
Thou shalt not link my awful Name
  With jest or word unholy.
And on the Day which I have named
  My own o'er earth and ocean,
Thy hand must rest—thy heart be tamed
  To meek and still devotion.
Honour *them* both who gave thee birth,
  For that which they have given;
Honour *them* too who watch on earth,
  That thou may'st wake in heaven.
Refrain thy hand from murderous dee
  Thy soul from sinful pleasure.
Though tempted by unlawful greed,
  Touch not thy neighbour's treasure.
Let truth in every gesture show,
  And peace and justice guide thee,
Till frailty shall not fear to go
  And weep her woes beside thee.
Let pure thoughts in thy bosom dwell,
  In love with angel pleasures.
Too freely wish thy brethren well
  To covet from their treasures.
And be it still thy crown of pride,
  And still thy life-long labour
To love thy God o'er all beside,
  And, as thyself, thy neighbour.

THE VOICE OF THE SANCTUARY.

How often, on the hill-top,
   Have I counted from above
The number of the churches
   Which bore witness of Thy love;
How many a dart of gladness
   Through my spirit Thou hast cast,
From Thy Tabernacles aiming,
   As all silently I passed.

And dost Thou not remember
   How at night I used to wake,
Sleep chased away by thinking
   Of Thee watching for my sake?
And hast Thou quite forgotten
   With what love I used to pine,
Till the morning light recalled me
   Back again unto Thy Shrine?

Ah! Love, the bliss is over
   Of such morning and such night;
If now my sleep is broken,
   'Tis with evil thoughts to fight;
And oft the morning summons
   Is so grudgingly obeyed,
That some holy meditation
   I must gather to my aid.

But ever on the hill-top,
   If I count them from above,
The number of the churches
   Can bear witness to Thy love:

Neither dryness nor temptation
  Shall e'er move me to despair,
While I think upon Thee, dwelling
  In Thy Tabernacles there.

SHADOWS ON OUR PATH.

How oft, in weariness and fear,
  I turn away my gaze,
While Thou dost lead me, step by step,
  Through Thine appointed ways:
I fain would keep the onward course,
  Yet shudder as I go,
Since, for the good I have not seen,
  I quit the good I know.

At times, a light upon my path
  From Thy dear smile comes down,
But ere I have enjoyed it half
  It changes to a frown:
At times, Thy voice, distinct and clear,
  Invites my steps to flee,
But when I would obey Thy call
  It sounds no more for me.

Where Thou art, my beloved God!
  In brightness or in gloom,
In happy church, or silent cell,
  Or weary working-room,
With all Thy glory round Thee shed,
  Or on Thy cross alone,
Speak to this heart what way Thou wilt,
  But make it all Thine own.

SAINT LEWIS AND THE FLOWERS.

Saint Lewis Bertrand entered, at the age of fifteen, the order of Friars Preachers. While waiting for this favour (delayed by various obstacles) his greatest consolation was to remain near the Dominican Convent at Valentia, occupied with the care of the garden. (Died 1581.)

It was a church-like garden, with its atmosphere of prayer,
The brethren walked deep musing through the silent pathways there ;
The flowers grew up in beauty, and the bird-notes sang in love,
And the bright, warm sky of summer, like a glory, shone above.

It was a church-like garden, on its noontide silence fell
The high and solemn music of the deep-toned convent bell;
And the chanting from the choir made a murmur in the air,
Which at matins or at vespers, seemed to people it with prayer.

There were eyes upon that garden, when the brethren little knew ;
There were hands that worked unwearied, where the beauteous roses grew,
There were thoughts that fed upon it, till its bloom appeared to be
A sacred thing to kneel before, a blessedness to see.

'Tis the young and ardent Lewis, of the brow serene and grave,
If he may not be their brother, he but asks to be their slave ;

And, like dew, upon the flowers' fall his tears without
 a sound,
For he envies their upspringing in that consecrated
 ground.

Oh! fair is the lone garden in its stillness and retreat,
But fairer the young spirit that upon its paths we meet;
And bright is every flower he sees opening to the sun,
But brighter *he* shall blossom ere his earthly work be
 done.

'Tis the young and holy Lewis—when the twilight
 shadow falls,
And the church is closed till morning, he lies hid
 within the walls;
And the midnight hours invite him, by their stillness
 and repose,
To recount unto his Saviour all the history of his woes.

Oh! fervent prayers are offered where the midnight
 hangs around,
And the tears of young St. Lewis fall like rain upon
 the ground;
But a deeper warmth shall reach him, and a brighter
 flame shall glow,
And his words shall dart like fire, where his tears are
 gushing now.

St. Dominic yet shall crown *him* who had clung to
 him so well,
Who had tracked his holy footsteps, and had kissed
 them where they fell,
Whom time could not outweary, and whom frowns
 could not offend,—
Who kept hoping to the latest, and kept loving to the
 end.

PAST AND PRESENT.

WHEN the shadows cover
   Drooping heart and wings,
And the day is over,
   How the night-bird sings!
While the sun was shining,
   He but felt the ray;
Now his secret pining
   Sings itself away.

Thus, my God! my Treasure!
   In Thy noontide gaze,
I but felt my pleasure,
   And adored Thy rays;
Now when gloom and sorrow
   All my soul o'ercast,
Some delight I borrow,
   Singing of the Past.

NAMES AT CONFIRMATION.

SAINT JOSEPH! Patron from my birth,
   And guardian of my vow,
My childish pride rebelled against
   What my heart longs for now;
For I refused the Name, because
   I heard so many say
That thou *shouldst* be my Patron Saint,
   Whose Feast was my birthday.

On which my busy pride began,
    In tempting hues, to paint
How every child was free to choose
    Her own sweet Patron Saint;
But *I*, because I chanced to see
    The light on one March day,
Could never pass from out the bounds
    Of thy paternal sway!

Then, urged by wayward fancies on,
    I set myself to see
If birthday right had not assigned
    Some other Saint to me;
And, when above the scene I saw
    Saint Patrick's octave shine,
My heart in secret formed the wish
    That Patrick's Name were mine.

Then all so fast, I seemed to see
    His guiding hand more fit
For me, whom Irish earth had formed,
    And Irish sunshine lit;
And, bolder grown in fancied right,
    My words began to be,
"I'll take Saint Patrick's Name, because
    He left the Faith to me."

But now I grieve—*not* for the Name—
    The glorious Name and dear!
But for the *will*, so early bent
    To pride and passion here;
For had my soul been free from such,
    I ne'er had hoped to pay
Saint Patrick's Name a tribute, in
    Saint Joseph's slighted sway!

SAINT JOSEPH.

When Mary on the dark earth trod,
With feet unsullied by its sod,
Who guarded her young life for God?
                        Saint Joseph.

When Mary heard her cousin's need,
And crossed the mountain-land with speed,
Who shared her generous thought and deed?
                        Saint Joseph.

When Bethlehem had no room to spare,
For Jesus or for Mary there,
Who cherished with a father's care?
                        Saint Joseph.

When Jesus on the Virgin's breast
Lay in His infant slumbers pressed,
Who worked in joy, that they might rest?
                        Saint Joseph.

When Mary, from her home exiled,
Fled sadly with her royal Child,
Who guided through the trackless wild?
                        Saint Joseph.

When Mary's Infant older grew,
And took His share of labour too,
Who set the tasks He longed to do?
                        Saint Joseph.

When Mary sought her Son in vain
With agonising heart and brain,
Who felt and shared her wordless pain?
                        Saint Joseph.

When his own parting hour drew nigh,
Who laid him down in peace to die,
With Jesus and with Mary by?
Saint Joseph.

And who can love the Virgin blest,
The God who slumbered on her breast,
Nor dearly love who loved them best?
Saint Joseph.

PURE GOLD FOR THE SHRINE.

Now, when His gracious call invites,
  Rise up, bound forth, and say—
The world with all its vain delights
  Shall leave my heart this day:
No more within that sacred spot,
  Where God hath fixed His home,
Shall idle dream or sinful thought
  To break His slumber, come.

Mine eyes, watch o'er His holy place,
  That none may pass within
To dim the sweet celestial grace
  Which He delights to bring.
My speech, by one sweet impulse stirred,
  Grow warm with love so dear;
Mine ears, shut out the lightest word
  Unfit for Him to hear.

My feet, His every call obey,
  His paths delight to tread;
My hands, be busy night and day,
  For those for whom He bled.

My soul, transformed by love divine,
   Embrace your glorious Guest,
And all your fears and joys consign
   To Him, within your breast.

A CRY IN TEMPTATION.

"Lord, save us, we perish."—Matt. viii. 25.

I NEED not fall, I need not fall,
Though earth and hell assail me all;
From heaven above I'm sure of aid,
Which soon will make my foes afraid.

From Heaven above, to meet my cry
Ten thousand Angels forth will fly,
Whose fiery words and arrows bright
Will shortly put my foes to flight.

If I should fail, if I should fail,
'Tis not because my foes assail;
No! Lord, the cause can only be
Because I do not cry to Thee.

Then make me breathe such ceaseless prayer
For grace and mercy everywhere,
That earth and hell shall fear to see
A soul that keeps so close to Thee.

ANGELS OF STRENGTH.

The Virtues! the Virtues! how grand is their sway,
Whom the thunder and tempest are bound to obey,
Who can lash the mad sea till her wild waters shriek,
Then snatch from her fury the helpless and weak.

On nights such as these, when the loud winds are high,
And the red lightnings dance through the air and the sky,
Let us think of poor mariners, tossed on the wave,
And beseech of the Virtues to succour and save.

Oh! kind are the Virtues, by sea and by land,
Though they ride with the scourge and the lash in their hand,
Dread foes to encounter, 'tis easy to see,
When you lean on the Virtues, what friends they can be.

But the friend of the Virtues must struggle and dare,
No pride must he foster, no vice must he spare;
Through the wild waves of passion, the torrent must stem,
By invoking the Virtues, and hearkening to them.

Dread Angels of courage, and grandeur, and force!
Incite to the goal, and defend on the course;
Impel where we ought, and dash down what we like,
Assist us to conquer, and force us to strike.

Defend from the storms that obey your control,
And preserve in the deadlier strife of the soul;
In the front of the danger be with us to cheer,
Crying—courage and safety, the Virtues are here!

FREEDOM.

Yes, Father, lift Thy hand of power,
   And let thy chastening rod
Prepare my soul for that dread hour
   When she must meet her God:
Let foes rush in on every side
   To torture and dismay,
But leave no stain unpurified
   For that avenging day.

O God! the boundless joy, to spring
   At death's first summons, free
From every vile and earthly thing,
   To Thy full court and Thee.
To suffer where Thy pangs have been,
   To smile where Thou art blest,
To know no weary space, between
   My labours and my rest!

THE FLIGHT INTO EGYPT.

Swift answering to St. Joseph's word,
   The Mother clasped her Child,
And silently, with bleeding heart,
   She bore Him through the wild.

What! though ten thousand Angels sang
   Round His celestial throne,
On earth He had no refuge, save
   In her kind arms alone.

She wept not for the friends she left,
   But few the poor can find;
She wept not for the shelter rude,
   So hastily resigned;

But how her streaming eyes o'erflowed
   To see the thankless lot
Of Him, who "came unto His own,
   And they received Him not."

How rushed her prophet-soul along
   To yet a future day,
When secret flight could snatch no more
   From bitter death away!

How closed her twining arms about
   The Child they *yet* could save,
From those who but his cradle sought
   To bear Him to His grave!

THE DEFENCE IN THE HALL.

O THOU weeping Flower! arise,
Every tear-drop in thine eyes,
All thy weight of trailing hair,
All thy perfumes lavished there,
And thine attitude of shame,
And Thy grief-convulsèd frame;
With the love that made thee strong
Thus to pass the jeering throng,
All thy spirit wrung and bowed
By the insults of the crowd;
Fearing lest *He* too might share
In the scorn that met thee there;
Fearing lest He should not see
All that He had wrought in thee,
And would turn with wrathful mien
From the prostrate Magdalene!

Oh! what language do they speak
To that silent Judge and meek,
Heeding more their mute appeal
Than the hot and angry zeal
Of the guests, who taunt thee so
With thine unforgotten woe;
Thus, to kneel one moment there,
Thou His very wrath didst dare;
Thus, to weep before His face
Thou didst court thine own disgrace.

Oh, lift up thine eyes to see
Brow that hath no frown for thee,
Eyes, that, conquered by thy tears,
Look not on thy sinful years:
Pause awhile,—before them all
He defends thee in the Hall!—
He! thy Saviour, turns to plead,
Stoops to bind His " broken reed !"
From thy fetters speaks release,
Bids thy spirit " go in peace,"
And with secret, sweet control,
Calms the tumult of thy soul.

WHEN TO SURRENDER AND WHEN TO HOLD FAST.

Oh! think how the Patriarch wrestled so long
  With the Angel he met on his way,
But when he had blessed him, he let him pass on,
  Nor asked for a further delay:
But the Spouse in the Canticles, clasping her Love,
  Would never permit Him to part,
Nor could all the rich blessings that rain from above
  E'er tempt her away from His Heart.

Thus does on-rushing circumstance meet us through life,
  With a blessing prepared to bestow,
And thus should we show ourselves bold in the strife,
  And insist on it ere we let go:
But the Ruler of circumstance finding at last,
  So fast should we spring to His call,
That, still clasping the loved One through sunshine and blast,
  We never may leave Him at all.

THE GIFT FOR THE GIVER.

Oh! not for this—to snatch from Him the treasure—
  Hath He that young heart blest with gift divine;
He hath not warmed it for the halls of pleasure,
  He hath not decked it for another's shrine.
Is it too much for Him—the Lord of Heaven!
  Without whose smile these very heavens were dim,
That His own gift should back to Him be given,
  That His own creature should belong to Him?

Oh, young and pure! to whose untroubled seeing
  All the wide world is clothed in rainbow light,
Think, who awoke in you this buoyant being,
  Think, who calls forth for you each fresh delight.
Clasp, if you will, the pleasures that He sends you,
  Where His own pathway was so cold and dim,
But clasp with them the Hand that thus befriends you,
  And taste your sweetest joy in thanks to Him.

Cry to the world, when artfully she presses
    To her light love or her bewildering strife,
"Not for your tinselled crowns, nor vain caresses
    Hath my Creater warmed me into life."
Turn your fresh hearts to this most faithful Lover,
    Ere the first glory of your youth be past;
And, oh! when shadows of the night fall over,
    How will He fold you to His own at last.

You who have wandered in the paths of pleasure,
    You who have sinned against the God of love,
Not with your miseries His mercies measure,
    For they are still His highest works above :
Fall at His feet with but one cry of sorrow,
    Ask Him to mark you for His own anew;
Soon will you bless Him for a brighter morrow
    Of hope and joy than ever dawned on you.

O my dear Lord! how was my wild youth wasted,
    Loved by a world that falsely spoke to me,
Till each new hour, as far from me it hasted,
    Bore the new impress of some wrong to Thee.
Oh, my sweet Love! how have I lost and left Thee,
    Thou who first formed me for Thyself alone ;
Of this poor heart too long have I bereft Thee,
    Now I would die to make all hearts thine own.

THE SPANISH LADY.

Too dear for earth the Maiden was,
    Who smiled like Saints above ;
Her beauty raised the soul to joy,
    And won the heart to love.

And she was watched by many an eye,
    And praised by many a tongue,
And hearts were even sick with fear
    Lest hers should not be won.

Too bright for earth the Maiden was,
    And shone like Saints above,
When calming fears that rose too high,
    And yielding love for love.

And once her plighted word was given
    And her full heart revealed,
She loved with that unswerving faith
    Which loyal natures yield.

What thought is in her brain to-night?
    What cloud is on her brow?—
A lovelier lot could maiden choose
    Than that before her now?

No blighting scorn has she to fear,
    No parent's frown to dread,—
Of noble lineage is the youth
    Whom she will shortly wed.

Of noble lineage is the youth;
    No lady in the land
Could say that he had dared too much,
    In seeking heart and hand.

Yet clouds are on the maiden's brow,
    And thoughts are in her eyes,
And there are questions in her heart
    To which her soul replies.

What stain upon his chivalry,
  What blot on his high vows,
That he must hear the *dowry* told,
  While waiting for the spouse!

Her tenderness, her purity,
  Her loftiness of soul—
Another love may answer them,
  But *that* is not their goal.

The burst of pain was over soon,
  In prayer the night went by;
No morning smile the maiden wore,
  But strength was in her eye.

Yet mournfully her footsteps fell,
  As to the Church she trod,
Where, in the still confessional,
  She bared her soul to God.

No cloud is on the maiden's brow,
  To hear the story told
That there is One who cares for her,
  And thinks not of her gold.

But softly do her tears come down,
  For never yet before
She felt how deep a blessedness
  To love what we adore.

She felt what heights of ecstasy
  The favoured soul must touch,
Who, though she lives and dies for love,
  Can never love too much

Who wakes to God at morning dawn,
   And rests in Him at night,
And never quits His folding arms,
   Nor wanders from His sight;

Who rests because He bids her rest,
   And works when He commands,
And serves Him with her beating heart,
   And with her busy hands;

Who feels that all which smiles below,
   And all which shines above
But witness to His excellence,
   And testify His love.

Her tenderness, her purity,
   Her loftiness of soul,
Her starry dreams of worshipping—
   Oh! *this* has been their goal!

A WORD FOR THE HOLY IMAGES.

The Images of Mary!
   Oh! guard them in your love,
Herself hath found a dwelling
   In the smiling Heaven above;
No more upon the dark earth
   Do her virgin footsteps tread,
But the Image of her beauty
   We can honour in their stead.

While the friend is in the chamber,
   On his image who would gaze?
Who would linger by the portrait,
   Could he look upon the face?
But, in long and pining absence,
   How it comforts us to show
All the love unto the picture,
   That the friend can never know.

But the Images of Mary
   Have a value far beyond;
She will know when we are faithful,
   She will bless when we are fond;
She will pay us for the homage,
   She will thank us for the care
That we lavish on her Image,
   As if she herself were there.

Oh! then light your waxen tapers,
   Bring your garlands to her shrine
Cast no slight upon her altars,
   Lest she take it for a sign
That herself hath scanty honour
   Where her colours can be sold,
And her Images surrendered
   As a lighter thing than gold.

Let them never, never tempt you,
   In "compassion for the poor,"
To be false unto her standard
   Who their every wound can cure;
All the gems of England's peerage,
   All the gold in England's hand
Could not match the smile of Mary,
   For the safety of our land.

Better see them pine in thousands,
    Both the aged and the young,
With her light upon their spirit,
    And her name upon their tongue,
With her mantle flung around them
    For a shelter from the blast,
Than behold their cheerless plenty
    If her blessed reign were past.

Oh, sweet and sacred Image
    Of my Mother and my Queen!
Still left to keep her impress
    On the earth where she has been.
Though I think and think for ever,
    I can never comprehend
How to desecrate the portrait
    And to venerate the friend.

If I think and think for ever,
    I can never understand
The daring of the spirit,
    Or the boldness of the hand
That can tear thee from thy holding
    In the happy school-room shrine,
Where the little children gather,
    Singing hymns to thee and Thine.

BREATHING TIME.

Like a tired child, upon Thy breast
How quietly I seem to rest,
And scarcely feel what pains oppress,
Because of all Thy tenderness.

And yet I know, while here I stay,
That there will come another day
When, seeming from Thy presence cast,
I'll feel the shock of every blast.

Oh! while these peaceful hours remain,
Prepare me for that burst of pain;
And when the maddening billows roar,
Oh! strengthen me to cling the more.

Prompt every word the lips shall say,
When the wild thoughts refuse to pray,
And bid the Sea-star shed her light,
Lest there should be a wreck that night.

O Father! it is hard to trace,
Thus resting in Thy dear embrace,
The sudden storm of gloom and woe
Which hurls me to the depths below;

Yet, then as now, Thine arms enfold,
Though mine lose all their power to hold;
And fast upon Thy Heart I stay,
Though hell would fain have torn away.

Ah! smite my falsehood, lash my guilt
By any sharpest scourge Thou wilt—
But though one arm be raised to kill,
Sustain me with the other still.

THE LOST TALISMAN.

There is a little purple flower
   Which, German legends tell,
Though low it grows, hath in its power
   A very potent spell;

If he who sees this purple flower
    Shall, stooping snatch it up,
A thousand sparkling gems will shower
    From out its fairy cup.

I like this legend passing well,
    And often pray to meet
The purple flower of potent spell
    Which groweth at the feet.
For *humble prayer*, as all may know,
    Such priceless treasure brings,
That though we seek it e'er so low,
    To find it makes us kings.

But, ah! success hath tempting power,
    And German legends tell
How many quit the purple flower,
    To watch the gems too well:
When with the faint forgotten bloom,
    The gems and all depart,—
Ah! need I point the moral home
    To any reader's heart?

WHAT MY ANGEL COULD DO FOR ME.

O MY Angel! Angel dear!
Furl thy wings a moment here,
Strike thy harp, until my own
Catch an echo from its tone.

Thou canst rule, and thou canst sing,
Thou art minstrel, thou art king;
Sing unto my ear, and then
Touch my lips to sing for men.

Thou hast many a song, I know,
Fit for us to hear below,
Songs of crownèd saints above,
Songs of wonder and of love.

Thou couldst tell of brows, by woe
Bowed unto the dust below,
Smiling now with radiance high,
Wearing rose-wreaths in the sky.

Thou couldst tell of martyred saints,
At whose pangs the spirit faints,
Joying now for all they bore,
Wishing they had suffered more.

Thou couldst tell of souls that weep,
In their prisons strong and deep,
Wondering if all friends forget
That they love and suffer yet.

O my Angel! Angel dear!
Still my loved companion here,
Tender father, faithful guide,
Friend for ever by my side.

Prince of Heaven! wert thou like me,
Would not this thy solace be,
In cold banishment, to sing
Of thy country and thy king?

Hear my prayers, and grant my boon,
Set my heart in perfect tune;
Bid my song gush forth, as free
As thy love rains down on me.

A PETITION TO SAINT ALPHONSUS.

Dearest Saint, so wise and bright,
  Shed your kind prayers over
Every single song I write
  For my royal Lover:
Every line of yours is warm
  With the strength of praying;
I want such another charm,
  Through my verses straying.

Father! both for love and light
  On your kind endeavour,
Every song this hand shall write,
  Shall depend for ever.
Writers seek in vain to move,
  Trusting thought and toil;
Tis the prayer of Faith and Love
  Must prepare the soil.

Will you not my Pleader be?
  I were weak without you;
You have been so much to me,
  'Tis no time to doubt you.
Make my writings like your own,
  Fenced by prayer still stronger;
May their work of love go on
  When I write no longer.

THE MERCY OF GOD.

'Tis the glow of His love which hath ripened the harvest,
    The dew of His pity that freshens the sod;
Then raise we an anthem, a heart-stirring anthem,
    And be its glad chorus—the Mercy of God.
Yes! sing for these mercies that never have tired,
    As fresh at this hour as when first they began,
Delighting the Saints, and amazing the Angels,
    Such wonders they work in the service of man.

'Twas the Mercy of God that tracked out that poor sinner
    Who tottered so long on the borders of hell,
When the sting of remorse which impelled to confession
    Left his soul just absolved, as the stroke of death fell.
'Tis the Mercy of God that hath snatched that sweet maiden
    From earth, while her footsteps in innocence trod:
The angels are glad, and the demons are wailing—
    Their web has been crossed by the Mercy of God.

'Tis the mercy of God which hath flung the gay sunshine,
    So warm, round the steps of these children at play;
The time may come on for the cloud and the tempest,
    But young hearts must gladden and bask in the ray.
'Tis the mercy of God that when tempests rush over,
    As mild as a mother, will look from above
To calm the first cry of their grief and their terror,
    And soothe all their sorrow with whispers of love.

'Tis the Mercy of God that when hopes are the highest,
　Doth dash, on a sudden, these hopes to the sod,
Lest pleasure begin to ensnare and mislead us
　From singing for ever the Mercy of God.
'Tis the Mercy of God that when life is the calmest,
　Doth wake up the sorrow which spurs us along,
Lest footsteps, delighted to tread amongst flowers,
　Should linger till summer was over and gone.

'Tis the Mercy of God that first drew us from nothing,
　To hang round this nothing its trophies of love;
Our beam in the night, and our shade in the sunshine,
　That ill may not reach us below nor above.
'Tis the Mercy of God sends the song to the poet,
　The quick-throbbing life to the heart-beat within;
'Tis the Mercy of God gives the longing to bless It,
　And teaches the spirit to love and to sing.

'Tis the Mercy of God, the enduring and patient,
　Which grieves to see any escape from its hold;
How hard must they fight, and how long must they struggle
　Who, madly resisting, keep out of its fold!
Then raise the glad song on the heights of the mountain,
　And let the gay chorus ascend from the sod,—
Our hope on the earth, and our home in the heavens,
　Our end and beginning—the Mercy of God!

DAILY COMMUNION.

While Thy desire is all on fire
    To eat this Pasch with me,
Shall I be led by slavish dread,
    From Thy good Pasch and Thee?

While Thou dost wait outside my gate
    And knock with patient mien,
Shall I delay the word to say
    Which bids Thee enter in?

Shall I resign this boon divine,
    In idle hope to grow,
When far from Thee, more fit to be
    Thy dwelling-place below?

Ah! Lord, if still so faint my will,
    While by Thy side I stand,
I dread to think how fast I'd sink
    Without Thy helping hand.

Nor would I stay one hour away,
    If every hour I could
Invite Thy rest within my breast,
    My own eternal Good!

No use can kill, no custom chill
    The daily joy to find,
The All I love below, above,
    In my own heart enshrined.

Yet, in this breast, Thou'rt less a guest,
    Than a dear Spouse to see,
All night and day, Thy will and way
    The only law for me;

And in my prayer, I less prepare
    Thy formal welcome here,
Than bid Thee come to Thy own home,
    And order Thy own cheer.

NATURE'S BOOK.

God alone! God alone! don't you hear them singing,
When throughout the summer air happy birds are
    winging?
God alone! God alone! don't you see it lying
In the dewy flower-cups when the day is dying?
Not a star upon the sky, not a wave upon the ocean,
With its clear and crystal light, or billowy emotion,
But is whispering of its God to all who love to hear
    it,
Preaching softly to the souls that draw for counsel
    near it.

Nature is an open book—God is writ within it,
Simple hearts and pious minds read His lessons in it;
Oh! bethink you ere you blot such fair leaves with
    error!
From sowing tares in God's own field shrink with
    wholesome terror.

Seek, for all your idle loves, songs that will befit
    them,
Sun and stars are fain to plead for the love that lit
    them;
Theirs is still the music true, yours the interruption,
Wresting from the truth itself falsehood and corruption.

THE LEGACY.

"*My little children, love one another.*"—*St. John.*

ALL yearning for his home of rest
  The great Apostle lay,
He who had leaned on Christ's own breast
  Before the mournful day;
He who had leaned on Christ's own Heart,
  And caught its sacred thrill,
With life's last effort, would impart
  Its loved injunction still.

" My little children, walk in love,
  This one command obey,
'Tis all the doctrine you can move
  These aged lips to say;
'Twas all I learned upon His Heart,
  Or gathered from His speech;
'Tis all my own shall e'er impart
  While I live on to teach.

" My little children, walk in love,
  By this shall all men know
That He doth rule your hearts above,
  When they are linked below.

My little children, walk in love,
    But in such love, as drew
Your Saviour from His Heaven above
    To bleed and die for you."

Yes! brethren, 'tis the one command
    Which Christ hath called *His Own*,
Hath left to every age and land,
    To garret, and to throne;
To children at the mother's knee,
    And men worn out with care;
A simple rule, which all may see
    Can no exception bear.

And if you say—I love my friend—
    Do not the heathens so?
But Christ His strengthening grace can send
    To make you love your foe:
And if you love the work He wrought
    When guilty man was lost,
How can you hate the soul He bought
    At such a fearful cost?

But when you love, remember yet
    What sort of love is due!—
The same which caused your God to set
    His Providence o'er you;
An active love, to aid and bless,
    A patient love to bear,
An humble love to cling no less
    Where nothing pays your care;

A constant love, through weal and woe
    To wear unchanging smile,
An ordered love, to guard below
    From every evil wile;
A love, which, born of God's command,
    To God alone doth tend,
And warms the heart, and fills the hand
    For foe as well as friend.

Oh! brethren, 'tis the one command
    Which He hath called *His Own*,
Hath left to every age and land,
    To garret and to throne;
To children at the mother's knee,
    And men worn out with care;
A simple rule, which all may see
    Can no exception bear.

TO THE LAMP BEFORE THE BLESSED SACRAMENT.

O HAPPY Lamp! that burns all day
Where my poor heart were fain to stay,
For ever to my God I pray
That He would make me like to you,
In death as blest, in life as true;
Companioned still by Angels there,
Fed with the oil of holy prayer,
A shining light for men to see,
And glorify my God in me.

A burning lamp before His throne,
To love and live for Him alone,
And then to die some happy day,
By that dear love consumed away.

ALL FOR LOVE.

Thou knowest 'tis not so much the fear
    Of purgatorial fires
That makes me wish to suffer here
    What Justice still requires;
But earth has been Thy trial-place,
    And, while on earth, I see
In every grief some tender trace
    And shadowing of Thee.

On earth did Mary bear her cross
    Through many a weary year;
On earth lived on in pain and loss
    Of all her heart held dear:
And still, with every pang below,
    To her kind arms I flee,
Remembering Mary felt the woe
    Whose shadow rests on me:

Yet work Thy will, Redeemer true,
    Howe'er my thoughts incline,
My heart's first wish is still to do
    That holy will of Thine:
But still, in patience, may I prove
    That I can always see—
'Tis sweet to suffer here, for love
    Of Mary and of Thee.

SAINTS AND SINNERS.

"Oh, but they were Saints!"

Say not they were *Saints*, and so
   Ran along the ways of God,
Heeding not if weal or woe
   Followed on the path they trod.
Say not they were *Saints*, and thus,
   Led by secret unctions on,
Scarce are models fit for us,
   Stumbling as we creep along.

Brethren, they were Saints, because
   Pain they bore and felt it too,
All for sake of keeping laws
   Made as well for me and you:
They were Saints by proper use
   Of the reason God has given,
Counting it as gain to lose
   Earth, whene'er it clashed with Heaven.

Saints had deadlier fight than we;
   Hell pursued with fiercer ire.
Satan does not leave those free
   Who still mock his foul desire.
Saints were saved by lengthened prayer,
   Knees bent trembling on the sod,
Feet that fled from every snare,
   Heart-cries piercing up to God.

Saints are they who know their task,
   Hold their ground by fighting firm,
Strength for life's long warfare ask,
   And await its destined term.

When the tempter seeks your door,
   Use the grace which God has given;
If 'tis scanty, ask for more,—
   You, too, shall be Saints in Heaven.

SPIRITUAL SCENERY.

Long ago the lofty mountains
   Lifted up my soul on high,
And the singing, sparkling fountains
   Gladdened heart and ear and eye;
And I loved the early flowers
   In the first clear light of spring,
And the warm, long summer hours
   With the shadows which they fling.
Now, 'tis not that nature loses,
   Still her face is wondrous fair,
Though my spell-bound soul refuses
   Over long to idle there;
But a mightier lure is lurking
   Far inside Cathedral wall,
And, where holy Church is working,
   I have nature, God, and all.
E'en when prayer absorbs no longer,
   And mine eyes begin to stray,
Prayer again wakes up the stronger
   For the scenes on which they stay.
Yon lone lamp, in still devotion,—
   Constant votaress at the shrine—
Calls forth every deep emotion
   Of this yearning heart of mine.

Crowds, that others deem distraction,
   Are a perfect joy to me ;
'Tis my spirit's strong attraction—
   Mission-time and jubilee.
Thronged confessionals delight me,
   For the grace that's teeming there;
Holy clamours but invite me
   To a more subduing prayer :
And, when at the Lord's own table,
   Crowding brethren round I see,
Law of love ! how well I'm able
   To take up thy yoke on me.
Sudden clash of beads behind me
   Gives my soul more joy to know,
Than the bird-notes used to find me,
   In the greenwoods, long ago :
And to see a young child kneeling
   By a holy image nigh,
Warms me with a sweeter feeling
   Than my brightest days gone by.
Still my spring-time lives for ever,
   Still my early joys pursue,
But their old shapes charmed me never
   With the heart-thrill of the new.
Enter in and gaze at leisure,
   Souls that loiter round the porch !
There is room for love and pleasure
   In the old Cathedral Church.

HERO WORSHIP

Had I not been a Catholic,
   What ever could control
The strong desire of worshipping
   Which triumphs in my soul?
My fancy would have built a shrine,
   As through the world I passed,
And there, before some idol vain,
   My very soul were cast.

Still, counting it the greater sin
   To look to them above,
I should have conned romances old
   For earthly lights to love;
And as unto the blessed Saints
   No homage I could yield,
I should have raised my heroes up
   From tournament and field.

Thus, leading far astray from God,
   The very gift He gave,
The strong desire of worshipping,
   Would hurt instead of save;
But now, unfearing, I kneel down
   Wherever God is found,
And love Him more, the more I haunt
   His consecrated ground.

Oh! pity them and pray for them
   Who cast the helps aside,
Which God, so sweet and merciful,
   Doth evermore provide.

Who, strait as is the way to Heaven,
   Would narrow it still more.
And make it all too thorny-strewn
   For any to pass o'er.

They cannot help, despite their will,
   The love which gushes forth,
When genius or nobility
   Is walking on the earth:
They cannot keep their neck so stiff
   But it must sometimes yield
To speakers in the council-room,
   Or leaders in the field.

But, keeping still their warmth and light
   For earthly uses all,
They offer God some lifeless thing
   Which "*reason*" they miscall;
And thus it is, so many pass
   From cradle on to grave,
Whose strong desire of worshipping
   Doth hurt instead of save.

MY GOD AND MY ALL.

When Thou comest thus to me,
I have all sweet names for Thee;
I can call Thee Father, Friend,
First Beginning, Latest End;
Brother, with Thy love untold,
Dearest Spouse, to have and hold;

But Thy sweetest name and best,
Thrilling far above the rest,
Leaving nothing in me free,
Drawing all my heart from me,
Through my whole of being wound,
In Thy name of GOD is found.

Of all love-words most divine,
Solely, truly, fully Thine;
Sounding for no other ear,
Thine alone this tone can hear:
Sweet as other names may be,
Still they make but part of Thee;
Friend Thou art, but Father too,
Spouse, and yet a Brother true:
When I say—MY GOD, I name
Every tie and every claim;
All my soul is swayed and stirred
By Thy own distinctive word;
All the wonders Thou hast wrought
With it rush upon my thought,
All the love-links Thou hast bound
Press me closer at the sound.

When I faint away with pain,
As my life revives again,
Ere my reason wakes at all,
'Tis upon MY GOD I call:
When I know no creature by,
Dimness in my brain and eye,
'Tis His name upon my lips
Draws me from my soul's eclipse;
And I live again to know,
If I stay or if I go,
In the lower or upper air,
Still MY GOD is everywhere;

And that love can hold its clasp
There, where reason has no grasp;
And all, *all* shall nothing be
That is not MY GOD to me.

MAY WREATHS.

OH, bring your wreaths of white and green,
    And bring your blue-bells gay,
And all for love of Mary, Queen,
    Who rules the month of May.
Exotics, nursed with cost and care,
    And field flowers fresh and sweet,
That rich and poor to-day may bear
    Their gifts to Mary's feet.

Laburnum, where it highest blows,
    Should in your garlands shine,—
The nearer to the sun it grows,
    The fitter for the shrine.
Let children cull the flowers that creep
    Like infants on the ground,
While striplings bold will lightly leap
    Where rarest wreaths are found.

Bring violets, mild as Mary's eyes;
    Unwearied all the day
They'll yield her up their fragrant sighs
    When we have turned away:

But let us beg before we go
    That such may intercede,
And while they thank for all we owe,
    Still press for all we need.

Lay heart's-ease on her altar too:
    What flower more fit to show
The peace that in our bosoms grew
    This Mother's love to know?
But here, be mindful how we take
    A firm resolve, to leave
Whate'er within our lives could make
    The heart of Mary grieve.

There's none but in his soul hath lit
    Some secret wish or prayer;
Then be it in his garland writ,
    For her to read it there;
That when she casts her gracious eyes
    Upon our tribute flowers,
From each and all a prayer may rise
    To this sweet Queen of ours.

Let all who will sweet hedge-wreaths weave,
    Their work shall none gainsay,
Nor rarest flowers shall have the leave
    To mock such wreaths to-day;
For wild flowers have a cause to plead,
    And well does Mary know
That time and care are all they need,
    Like garden gems to grow.
So bring your wreaths of white and green,
    And bring your blue-bells gay,
And all for love of Mary, Queen,
    Who smiles on beauteous May.

SAINTED SISTERS.

They are twins in glory, sister lights above,
Two bright stars of Heaven, linked in bliss and love:
Both from childhood holy, both by sorrow tried,
Both shall wear their laurels, reigning side by side.

Time on earth divided,—one* had passed to God
Ere her saintly sister† through life's desert trod;
But their virgin footsteps left so like a trace,
That their Spouse hath crowned them in the same bright place.

And, as I gaze upward on that vision fair,
A sweet younger sister‡ still comes smiling there:
One who tracked their footsteps with a heart as true,
One who died a daughter of Saint Dominic too.

Our bright Rose so radiant, in her trancèd prayer,
All might see the dwelling of the Godhead there:
Our glad Rose, so circled by the smile of God,
Wonders bloomed around her wheresoe'er she trod.

Oh, my sainted Sisters! from your blissful seat,
See my poor heart weeping sadly at your feet:
'Tis the same white tunic I am called to wear,
'Tis the same dark mantle must protect my prayer.

---

* Saint Agnes of Montepulciano, Virgin of the Order of St. Dominic (Died 1317.)
† Saint Catherine of Siena, Virgin of the same Order. (Died 1380.
‡ Saint Rose of Lima, V. (Died 1617.)

Fain my steps would follow where your own have passed,
Fain my life show traces that on yours 'tis cast.
Still so weak to suffer, still so slow to do,—
Aid me, crownèd Sisters, to grow like to you.

INTERCESSION OF THE THRONES.

Would you calm a troubled spirit?
   It is well the heart to lift
To the Angels who inherit
   Peace, as their peculiar gift:
Biting cares, how quick they soften
   For the soul who, through her groans,
Begs the longed-for respite, often
   From the calm and cloudless Thrones!

Think how blest that choir reposes
   Wherein God doth, resting, share
His full peace, which still discloses
   Some diviner sweetness there!
Would you rule the heart's affection
   Till no wandering wish it owns?—
Kneeling, crave the sweet protection
   Of the rapt and sinless Thrones.

See what cherub eyes are blazing
   Brightly in the ranks above,
Fearless through the light upgazing
   Where the burning seraphs love.
Thus, where God hath fixed His station,
   Love the perfect wisdom crowns,
But that wisdom's first foundation
   Is the peace-gift of the Thrones.

When, at rest from low desires,
   Hearts reflect the Heaven above,
Light shines forth, and kindling fires
   Spread the burning reign of love;
But while still in chains we languish,
   Seeking respite from our groans,
Sweetly through the bosom's anguish
   Steals the whispering of the Thrones.

ON THE DEATH OF A YOUNG FRIEND.

SHE clung to life as I to death,
And yet she died in hope and faith
And love, although she wept to go
From many that she loved below.

Her struggle was to turn away
From all that cheered life's closing day,
To quit familiar word and face,
And pass into an unknown place.

My struggle is to bear the strife
Of cold and uncongenial life,
Through peril's hour to watch and wake,
And fear at every step I take.

To see the longed-for death draw nigh,
Prepare to strike, then pass me by;
And weaker, wearier than before,
Take up my cross of life once more.

O God! who made her strong to die
While life was warm in heart and eye,
Grant me to live resigned and meek,
Though death be all the good I seek.

THE STRANGER.

Oh! think on that moment so sad and so thrilling,
　When time, spurring onward, is asked for in vain,
When death is at hand with its aspect so chilling,
　And God and His judgments are all that remain;
When life with her pleasures, so vain and so fleeting,
　In hues of the rainbow no longer is decked,
And the fear-stricken soul is bewildered at meeting
　The moment she never could bear to expect.

Oh! think on that death which comes sooner or later
　To all who are born to this region below;
Your bliss may be great, and your hopes may be greater,
　But short is the triumph if death be your foe:
Now time is your own, and now grace is not wanting,
　Yet tremble, poor trifler! each instant you lose,
For death, icy death, is a niggard in granting
　The graces which life has been wont to abuse.

THE SUN-FLOWER.

The Sun-flower smileth to the ray,—
　Why, so should you or I!
We all rejoice in our own way
　To see the sun go by;

But much I praise that constant flower,
   Because I never knew
Her turn aside, in gloomy hour,
   Some meaner light to view.

Beloved God! when summer hour
   Thy beam of beauty brings,
My sun-touched soul hath little power
   To show how fast she clings;
But when Thy smile is turned away,
   Oh! mayest Thou ever see
Thy Sun-flower faithful to the ray
   Which lights her life from Thee.

DARKEST BEFORE DAWN.

Deep in the shadows of my room,
In stillness, loneliness, and gloom,
I live enclosed as in a tomb.

My strange disease has scared away
Familiar sound and cheerful ray:
'Tis night with me the live-long day.

The words which comfort would impart
Shoot such a terror through my heart,
In pure compassion friends depart.

And when, a living sound to hear,
I fain would speak to my own ear,—
At my own voice I shake with fear.

So loathsomely my life-blood goes,
As if recounting all my woes,
It chills and curdles, more than flows.

What a fierce torment she can be,
Imagination proves to me
Who but her hideous nightmares see.

Words, thoughts, and deeds that once seemed good,
Have now become a monster brood
Of ills, too clearly understood.

Sharp, fiery pains like arrows fly,
And as they strike in passing by,
I hear my own affrighted cry.

Yet, Lord! through all, how faith can see
That every blow is struck by Thee,
And struck in changeless love to me.

If light and bird-notes through my room
Should chase away the wintry gloom,
My thoughts were farther from the tomb.

If friends had from the first been free
To enter in and speak with me,
My hope had ne'er so grown to *Thee*.

And had Thy sweet, celestial light
Remained to gild and bless the night,
I ne'er had learned how Prayer can fight.

Then welcome! every sharpest pain
Which comes to cleanse the hidden stain,
Or plant one joy that will remain.

DAILY BREAD.

If I should kneel a hundred years in humble prayer to Thee,
I could not merit one small pain of all that rain on me:
'Tis Thy free love, from day to day, pours out the tide anew;
May mine look up in thankfulness, where endless thanks are due.

I seem like one quite tired of pain, and wearied out with woe,
In utter weakness sinking down at each succeeding blow;
But still my soul cries out in joy, "The stripes which come from Thee
Are sharp unto Thy foes and mine, but very dear to me."

I know the seeds of heavenly bliss are in the pains of earth;
I know that joys which never die from these short pangs have birth;
I know that many an earth-stained soul goes smiling to the grave,
Bewildered in a maze of joys, whom tears alone could save.

And, oh! when turning back to trace my own dark page once more,
What grace could ever warm my heart till pain had gone before?

Of every good has sorrow been the harbinger to
    me,—
And shall I wear a graceless frown her dear old
    face to see?

O pitying God! O gracious God! smite on and do
    not spare;
But wed to the strong grace of pain the saving grace
    of Prayer;
Then earth and hell may rage in vain; how fierce
    soe'er they be,
"Incline unto my aid, O God!" is shield enough for
    me.

SAINT PIUS V.

Saint Pius V. obtained the success of the Christian arms at the battle of Lepanto by means of prayer, and chiefly that of the Holy Rosary. (Died 1572.)

Thy life is all so lightly sketched,
    That no distinctive seal
I meet upon thy history
    For wandering song to steal.

But much my spirit joys to find
    Thee true to every call,
And rising still from rank to rank,
    And shining through them all.

The virtues of the studious child,
    And of the still recluse
Were first to charm thy youthful heart
    And serve thine early use.

But sterner work remained to do,
   And soon I see thee take
Thy place in Church and Council high,
   For thy great Master's sake.

And when the triple crown was set
   Upon thy brow, began
A wider course of dauntless good
   And daring love for man.

And still thy name is twined about
   The sacred conquest, wrought
When Beads above the banner hung,
   While Christian heroes fought;

And Moslem arms, beneath the force
   Of all-prevailing prayer,
Were humbled by such rude defeat
   As taught them to despair.

Again, when cruel foes would fain
   Thy precious life destroy,
A poisoned image of thy God
   They impiously employ.

They knew how oft these sacred feet
   Were pressed beneath thy lip,
And trusted in that loving kiss
   The fatal draught 'twould sip;

But, ah! for once, thy Lord repels
   The touch of thy embrace,
And quickly draws the poisoned feet
   From thy uplifted face.

And here I cast aside the pen
    Which now no more can say,
Because I scarcely know thee yet
    To whom I sing and pray.

Though much I thank thy kindly aid,
    Which set my fancy free,
To twine the few vague thoughts I had
    In one wild wreath for thee.

THE WITHERED FLOWER.

BEFORE the Virgin's altar
    A young man bent in prayer,
And laid down for his offering
    A withered May-flower there.

But there was one beheld him,
    Who whispered in his ear,
" The purse of gold thou bearest,
    Were it not better here?

" Our high and holy Mother,
    Small need of gifts hath she,
Yet what thou hast most precious
    Would thy best offering be."

" Then," said the youth, faint smiling,
    " That branch was offering fit,
For never miser loved his gold
    As I have treasured it."

And he laid the purse so weighty
   Down on the Altar-stone,
But counted for his *sacrifice*
   The withered leaves alone.

"SALUS INFIRMORUM."

GIVEN o'er by human skill and art,
   Given up by human care,
Our Lady of the Sacred Heart,
   To thee I turn my prayer:
Physicians read my hopeless state,
   And sadly turn aside
From pangs they cannot mitigate,
   And tears I cannot hide.
There is no help, in earth or Heaven,
   Thy word cannot bring near;
Long have I suffered, wept, and striven,—
   Then, Help of Christians, hear.

Strength for the failing, fainting limb,
   Rest for the troubled mind,
Courage to watch and wait for Him
   Who healeth lame and blind;
Peace where the raging passions rise,
   Hope where despair makes way,
Light for the dark and sullen skies
   That seem bereft of day.
Thou swayest the Heart of Christ in Heaven
   Thou art the Mother-Maid;
Long have I suffered, wept, and striven,—
   Most potent Virgin, aid.

Given o'er by human skill and art,
  Given up by human care,
I turn me to that Mother-heart
  Which never said—despair!
I lay me in thy sacred arms,
  I kiss thy sacred hands,
I pray thee calm these vain alarms
  By thy most sweet commands.
Through thee can strongest chains be riven,
  Through thee do combats cease;
Long have I suffered, wept, and striven,—
  O Lady! give me peace.

MUSIC ON THE MOUNTAIN.

This poem refers to a vision in which an Angel foretold to Blessed Henry Suso all the spiritual sufferings he was to endure for the perfect sanctification of his soul, notwithstanding the wonderful corporal mortifications he had undergone for twenty-two years. (Died 1565.)

"Now, Henry, lift thine eyes upon
  The starry heaven above,
For *there* is writ in prophecy
  Thy martyrdom of love;
As countless as these starry rays,
  Thy trials shall rush forth,
And, like the stars, their magnitude
  Be hidden from the earth."

Oh! how the *human* shrank before
  The future thus laid bare,
As all its secret horrors seemed
  To crowd upon him there!

For, like the sunny child who thinks
    The world is made for play,
In Suso's heart the human stirred,
    As innocently gay.

But fast he kept the rugged path,
    And, when upon the height,
He breathèd forth in human voice
    Angelical delight;
And sweeter stole the music
    Of his wisdom-breathing words,
Than the fragrance of the flowers
    Or the singing of the birds.

FIREWORKS.

LIKE the rocket which shoots from the earth to the sky,
Whose blaze is the brightest when ready to die,
Should the life of a poet unswervingly be
One fearless upspringing from nature to Thee.

Like the blaze of a rocket consumed by its light,
Shooting forth but for others its sparkles so bright,
Should the heart of a poet contentedly live,
Uncheered by the gladness 'tis destined to give.

But the rocket has only to shine and to soar
For one moment of radiance, and then is no more,
While the poet drags onward through wearisome years,
To the sound of his music, the weight of his tears.

Yet chide not, poor minstrel, the sorrows that bring
The soul-searching music to heart and to string;
But, grieving and singing, pass on to the shore,
Where song is eternal, and sorrow no more.

THE SHRINE OF SAINT JAMES.

O Saint! made perfect, by the longing
    Of great and unachieved desires
Around thy pathway ever thronging,
    Thy heart consuming in their fires!
Who, dying ere thy laurels grew,
    Dost wear no less thy crown in Heaven,
Since, what in life thou couldst not do,
    (Such scanty time to thee was given),
By favour of the will divine,
    In death itself thou dost as surely,
With miracles around thy shrine,
    Attracting men to live more purely,
Converting thousands to the faith,
    By signs and wonders gathered to thee,—
Apostle less in life than death,
    And crowned for souls that never knew thee.
'Tis sweet to see thee throned above,
    In robes of such undying splendour,
Whose works were measured by the love
    Which only longed the works to render:
'Tis sweet for captives, fettered down
    By chains that sickness forges ever,
To know that zeal can win her crown,
    Though from her labours forced to sever.

WHY DO WE KNEEL TO HER?

How do we feel to her?
Why do we kneel to her?
What shall I say to them—tempting me so?
   If we should kneel and pray
   All the long night and day,
Worthy to breathe her name ne'er could we grow.

   Wreaths may be twined for her,
   Life be resigned for her,
Eyes yield the light of day hers once to view,
   Minstrels may sing her name,
   Orators preach her fame,—
All shall have done for her less than her due.

   Think of the soul that first
   Saint on existence burst!
Pure, and adoring each life-breath she drew;
   Ne'er the least shade of sin
   Crept her young dawn within,
But, with her growing life, grace ever grew.

   Think of the God at rest,
   Hid in her virgin breast,
Pouring His life through hers all through His stay;
   Feeding the flame still more,
   Rising so high before,—
Spending His love on her, day after day.

   Think on the life she led,
   Deep in the lowly shed,
Breathing His atmosphere, drinking His grace,
   Catching His looks and sighs,
   Bathing her heart and eyes
In the meek Heaven of His words and His face.

　　　　Think on the woeful day,
　　　　When on His Cross He lay,—
What can be given *her*, standing close by,
　　　　Worthy to pay her loss,
　　　　There by that blood-stained cross,
Watching His agony—seeing Him die?

　　　　Think of the FLAMES that brought
　　　　Wonders so freely wrought,
Where, in the "Upper Room," she too would pray:
　　　　Long have *we* lost her trace,
　　　　Far on the heights of grace,
Yet from the Infinite drank she that day.

　　　　Why do we kneel to her?
　　　　How do we feel to her?
Why should I answer you, tempt as you dare?
　　　　All through my words, I grieve
　　　　For the poor trace they leave
Of the rich arguments prompting our prayer.

THE CONTEST.

SAINT FRANCIS and Saint Dominic were discoursing
　　on their way,
When from a neighbouring convent came the brethren
　　forth, to say
How the well, which lay beside it, no refreshing
　　draught could bring,
For the salt and brackish waters still seemed poisoned
　　at the spring.

So they prayed the holy Fathers that their blessing might be laid
Upon the loathsome waters, till in healthfulness they played;
For they knew their sway was mighty o'er nature and her laws,
And they trusted kind compassion, then, might advocate their cause.

Then spake our holy Father, and he prayed that they might bring
A vessel full of water from the salt and brackish spring;
And when the word was taken, and the monks had drawn it up,
He turned him to Saint Francis for his blessing on the cup.

But Saint Francis, in his meekness, only made the one reply,
"Be *thy* blessing laid upon it, thou art greater far than I;"
And with loving words and humble to each other did they pray,
Till for love and sweet obedience, holy Dominic first gave way.

Saint Dominic blessed the waters, and their loathsomeness was healed,
And a wholesome draught and pleasant ever after did they yield;
And Saint Francis, in his meekness, went exulting on his way,
For he heard the monks conversing on Saint Dominic's work that day.

But methinks our Father Dominic left a lesson for
    his own,
That in virtue's self they grudge not to behold them-
    selves outdone,
But, through love and sweet submission, ever hold
    themselves resigned
To yield the palm to others with humility of mind.

THE COMMUNION OF SAINTS.

How the Saints have loved each other!
    Never dreaming that they saw
But a sister or a brother
    With such sweet and holy awe;
Still, each other's virtues seeing,
    Still, unmindful of their own;
All in love with one bright Being,
    Seeking guide-stars to His throne.

How the Saints have thrilled each other
    With their instincts swift and true,
Each heart sharing with the other
    All it longed for, felt, or knew!
Glad or sad, for ever keeping
    One sublimest end in view;
Never changing, never sleeping,
    As your earthly friendships do.

For the Saints, what joyful meeting
    In God's own eternal day,
Each again some loved one greeting
    As a beacon of his way!
There with rapture undivided,
    Never more to range or roam,
How they bless each ray that guided
    To their far, eternal Home!

THE POWER OF ART.

Oh, gentle Art! which first was given
To woo with genial breath for Heaven,
How much they wrong thy truth and worth
Who bind thee in the chains of earth!

Sweet Music! meant to echo here
Such strains as are to Angels dear,
'Tis sad to hear thy rippling-flow
Invite to meaner joys below.

Dear song! with all thy wondrous power
O'er every age and every hour,
Why must we teach our hearts to be
As aliens from thy haunts and thee?

'Tis sad on pictured walls to trace
No pure design, no saintly face
To read its lesson from the skies,
And look its Heaven on wandering eyes!

Sad, that the power of Art must make
A snare at every step we take,
And the bright handmaid sent to free,
Our first and last enslaver be!

Oh! if the minstrel would but breathe
His strains for an eternal wreath!
Oh! if the painter caught his light
From Bethlehem's cave or Thabor's height!

If eye and ear were sweetly wooed
Through forms of beauty on to good,
Did trace of Heaven, in sketch or song,
To every Christian home belong;

Did youth grow up with heart and sense
Still bathed in holiest influence,
Where every lure of sound and sight
Charmed from the wrong path to the right:

How many a heart, which earth has bound
Her most unholy fetters round,
On joyous wing had soared above,
And sought its Heaven in Christ's dear love!

Ah! your vain joys and pictures bright
Cast on this world deceitful light,
And, in the heart's unguarded hour,
Feed its young passions into power.

Build for our homes a Christian Art,
To raise and not enslave the heart:
Stay not our course, as on we steer,
With light that makes temptation dear.

Let light meet Light,—let Art be given
To Him who gave, to God in Heaven;
With Angel forms the sense control,
And preach in music to the soul.

FOR MY DEAR MUSIC-MASTERS.

'Tis all because of the Angels bright
I'm ready to sing both day and night,
Still weaving music, and catching light
   From the Angel forms around me.

Oh! kind are the Angels both night and day;
Since first my spirit began to pray,
From them to gather a passing lay,
   What numberless lays they've found me!

Then sing for the Angels both night and noon,
In bleak December and sunbright June;
Their hearts and harp-strings are aye in tune,
   And their mantle of song around them.
Oh! list to the Angels both noon and night,
For their music utters a secret bright,
And it lifts the soul, with a full delight,
   To the Master who taught and crowned them.

CRIES TO GOD.

CLASP my heart to Thine own;
Bind my soul to Thy throne;
Let me not weep alone,
          Far from Thee.
Look on my weary brow;
Think on my ready vow;
Lord! there is none but Thou
          Canst comfort me.

Far from Thy courts I stray,
Weeping my soul away;
Oh! for one gentle ray
          Warming my tears!

Thou art a mighty God:
Under Thy chastening rod,
Prostrate on earth's dull sod
    My life appears.

Let our tears mingle there;
In Thy pangs let me share;
Ever this constant prayer
    Waileth to Thee.
Oh! how I thirst and pine
For one low word of Thine,
Answering back to mine,
    Speaking to me.

God of my inmost soul,
Centre, and spring, and goal,
Thou who canst all control!
    Why dost Thou go?
Wouldst thou be missed?—Thou art,—
God of this longing heart,—
Missed in its every part,
    Well dost Thou know.

Oh! turn again to me;
Think how I yearn for Thee;
Think what my life must be;
    Pity and see.
See Thy poor slave, O God!
Heart-humbled on the sod,
Kissing Thy chastening rod,
    Crying to Thee.

HOPE FOR THE VALIANT.

"Do not consider me that I am brown, because the sun hath altered my colour."—Cant. i. 5.

Oh! fear not, though dark be the face that I show,
'Tis My love in its ardour hath altered it so;
The light of the morning was pleasant and fair,
But the heat of the noontide is scorching to bear.

No, fear not the gloom of My Features to see,
Their shadow is only a shelter for thee;
But still, if in terror to see them o'ercast,
Come, hide in My Heart till the danger is past.

In "the dens of the lions" thy strength I would prove,
On "the mounts of the leopards" I crown those I love:
But I shield in the peril, and save in the strife,
And I wake from the death-throes to gladness and life.

Yet, jealous My Heart is, and hard is My Hand,
The more Thou dost yield Me the more I demand;
"Put My seal on thy arm and My seal on thy soul,"
For I hold he gives nothing who gives not the whole.

But I give, for her guerdon, such love to My own
That "seas cannot quench it, nor floods cannot drown,"
Till giving for ever,—of all things bereft,
She thinks she gave nothing—when nothing is left.

THE LOSS OF THE CHILD JESUS:

Oh! think not that the martyrdom
   Of chill suspense was spared
To her, who every crown has won,
   And every sorrow shared;
But weep above the doubts which fast
   Her soul began to rack,
When, missing her sweet Son, she asked
   If e'er He would come back.

In love she was so worshipping,
   In spirit so subdued,
So trembling was her guardianship
   Of such a priceless good,
That through her stainless bosom shot
   A pang of terror wild,
Lest she had sinned unwittingly,
   And so had lost her Child.

And then His fair humanity,
   Though He was God in all,
That frail and childlike form, alas!
   What woes might not befall?
And He for this had trusted thee!
   O Mary, Mother dear,
Thy dolours meet thee everywhere,
   Thy martyrdom was here.

THE OLD CHURCH AT LISMORE.

Old Church, thou still art Catholic, e'en dream they as they may,
That novel rites and worship here have swept the old away:

There is no form of beauty, reared by nature or by
    art,
Which preaches not God's simple truth to man's
    adoring heart.

In vain they tore the altar down, in vain they flung
    aside
The mournful emblem of the death which our sweet
    Saviour died;
In vain they left no single trace of Saint or Angel
    near,
For spirits pure still haunt the ground, and to the
    soul appear.

I marvel oft, in scenes like these, that coldly they
    can pray,
Nor hold sweet commune with the dead who once
    knelt down as they,
Yet *not* as they, in sad mistrust of their own kind—
    for, oh !
They looked in hope to their own Saints, these dead
    of long ago.

And then the churchyard, soft and calm, spread out
    beyond the scene,
With sunshine warm and soothing shade, and tears
    upon its green ;
Ah! though their cruel church forbid, are there no
    hearts will pray
For the poor souls that, trembling, left the cold and
    speechless clay?

My God ! I am a Catholic, I grew into the ways
Of Thy dear Church since first my voice could lisp a
    word of praise,

But oft I think, though my first years were taught
 and trained to wrong,
I still had learned the one true faith from nature's
 thrilling song :

For still, whenever dear friends die, it is such joy to
 know
They are not yet beyond the care that healed their
 wounds below ;
That we can pray them into peace, and speed them to
 the shore
Where clouds, and cares, and thorny griefs will chill
 their hearts no more.

The gentle saints, so meek below, so merciful above !
The glorious Angels watching still, with such untir-
 ing love !
The Virgin Queen of Heaven, too, with all her
 Mother's care !
Who prays for earth, because she knows what break-
 ing hearts are there.

Oh ! let us loose no single link that our dear Church
 hath bound,
To keep our hearts more close to Heaven, on earth's
 ungenial ground,
But trust to saint and martyr yet, and o'er less hal-
 lowed clay,
Long after we have ceased to weep, kneel faithfully
 to pray.

So shall this Isle for us be still the sainted as of old,
Where hymn and incense rise to Heaven, and holy
 beads are told ;
And e'en the land they tore from God through years
 of crime and woe,
Instinctive with His truth and love, shall breathe of
 long ago.

THE SWEETNESS OF SERVING GOD

Could you but know, could you but know
   How sweet it is to stay
In God's own loving arms at night,
   And do His work all day;
What happy minds the holy have
   When most they seem in pain,
And what a load the sinner bears,
   However great his gain;

How willingly, how fervently,
   You'd all kneel down and pray,
That Christ would lift His hands to bless
   Your little band to-day;
That Christ would keep you while you live,
   And watch you when you die,
And save you from this cold, false world,
   For His own Home on high.

FIAT.

Some watch and weep while others sleep,
   Some work while others pray;
Some count the flight of wintry night,
   Some welcome in the day.

Be mine the stand which Thou hast planned,
   The fight Thou dost decree,
My only view, Thy will to do,
   My course, to follow Thee.

OUR BEST FRIEND.

If their own faith but *lived* in men,
This earth were Paradise again;
For what hath Heaven itself more dear
Than the good God who dwelleth here,
With greater miracle of love,
Than in the glorious courts above?

At night, to feel with joyful thrill,
That His true love is watching still,
To rest beneath His kindly care
Through dreams that scarcely break our prayer;
And, when the morn looks bright above,
To bless Him for His sleepless love.

For evermore our hearts to rest
In the great Heart that loves them best:
To make our daily wants and cares
The subject of our daily prayers,
Till every need is clearly shown,
And every feeling all His own.

With the same love to clasp His cross
In bitter grief or trivial loss;
To trust His arm for great and small,
Still crying to the Lord of all—
"Behold my will prepared to do,
But, oh! my strength must come from You."

And most of all, no love to own
Which centres not in this alone,
Till in His Heart the tie be found
That all the rest must twine around,
And the one sun that warms below
Be the dear God who loves us so.

Oh! would you rend your earthly chain
With most of joy and least of pain?
Kneel by the altar where His love,
Kinder than on its Throne above,
Lets not His majesty appear,
Lest His poor children faint with fear.

There you will smile to see them fall,—
These mighty fetters one and all,
To leave you free and joyful too,
To live for Him who died for you :
Almost before we seek a grace,
We find it in that holy place.

Oh, my dear God! who built for men
Such earthly Paradise again,
Still charm us to Thy holy ground
Till our one joy is in it found,
And the one pain we fear to bear—
Privation of Thy Presence there.

THE VIGILS OF SAINT DOMINIC.

Of all the fair traditions that come floating from the past,
With the dear name of Saint Dominic like a halo round them cast,

There's none that leaves my spirit with his kindness
   so impressed,
As his watch of love and pity while the brethren were
   at rest.

His eyes were still unsleeping, as at night he went
   to pray
In the Church, for thus he rested from the labours
   of the day;
But he often left the altar, with his meek and silent
   tread,
To seek out each sleeping brother and to pray above
   his head.

He signed the cross upon him for a blessing and a
   prayer,
And he sprinkled holy water that no evil thing might
   scare,
Then silently departed, to the church again to glide,
Till the bell, with its loud pealing, brought them all
   unto his side.

At night when I am wakeful, I often seem to see
Our holy Father Dominic, as he looketh down on
   me,
And I think his word from Heaven, if in trustfulness
   I pray,
Will be like the holy water to keep evil things away.

Our own dear Father Dominic! may the kindness
   of your gaze,
In the daylight and the twilight, shed a blessing on
   our ways,
To cheer us in the danger, and to guard us from the
   foe,
With the same kind heart above us that you used to
   have below.

CHOOSE WISELY.

Would you be a hero?—'tis a noble aim,
Through the great King's service lies the road to fame:
Wounds are sure of healing suffered for His love,
While undying honour waits on them above.

Would you be a merchant?—I will not gainsay;
Heap your gains together in a lawful way:
Think what wealth is surest; trade if trade you must,
But in gold and jewels, not in chaff and dust.

Are you but a maiden dreaming how to love?—
List the open secret of the courts above:
Mark the daily wonder of the shrines below,—
God is not the Lover, maiden, to forego.

THE SACRAMENTS.

The Sacraments! the Sacraments! how quietly they keep
Embosomed in the Holy Church, unconscious and asleep,
Till wakening at some human need to potency and might,
They leap into the field at once and gird us for the fight.

Fair sacrament of Baptism—she meets us at our birth
And greets us with the smile of Heaven in welcoming to earth.

Then, when again in sinful plight we knock at mercy's
    door,
Comes Penance from her hiding-place, and opes to us
    once more.

And, as our growing passions crave the food they
    must not take,
The Eucharist is ready there, the spirit's thirst to
    wake,—
To wake, and still to satisfy, till all our wishes rest,
And feed upon their dearest joy, when God is in our
    breast.

But still, because the traitor world so many a snare
    hath set
To force us from the way to Heaven, by mockery or
    threat,
The holy Confirmation stands to light a deathless
    flame,
And bids us, like Christ's soldiers all, to glory in His
    name.

And when the world is fading off, and friends begin
    to glide
About the sick, with anxious looks they cannot always
    hide,
When the sunk heart is faint to think of what may
    soon be nigh,
Comes Extreme Unction tenderly, and tells us how to
    die.

But long ere life hath loosed its hold, when first the
    man looks round
Upon the world's great battlefield, to choose his van-
    tage ground,

Two Sacraments stand mutely by, and, his election
    made,
Its guardian spirit smiles on him and proffers him
    her aid.

If in the world his calling be, to use as using not,
To live unlike to other men, yet share their common
    lot,
To choose one partner on his course and never swerve
    again,
With Matrimony comes the grace which he has need
    of then.

Where Angel voices sweetly pierce through all the
    din of life,
Where holy Church looks forth to charm to her thrice
    hallowed strife,
Where the young spirit burns to face rough ways
    which Christ hath trod,
By Holy Orders power is wrought to do great things
    for God.

And so, in every guise they come, at home in smiles
    or tears,
With crowning for our happiness, and soothing for
    our fears;
How well they know each secret shade where light
    is to be flung!
How well they know each silent cell where hymns are
    to be sung!

How matchless is their eloquence, how fast their work
    they do!
No missioner was ever sent so fearless and so true;

They win, they awe, they influence, they quicken and
    control,
They cast their spells about the sense, and triumph
    in the soul.

The Sacraments! the Sacraments! seven champions
    of our way,
Seven beacons on our pilgrimage, to light us lest we
    stray!
How calmly would our lives go past, how sweetly
    would we die
If we but came for oil to them when our own lamps
    run dry!

GOLD OR LEAD.

O Lord! where are Thy "chains of gold
    Inlaid with silver" bright?
Those leaden fetters on my soul
    Weigh heavily to-night:
No light upon my spirit falls,
    Descending from above;
The captive of dull pain I seem,
    And not of smiling love.

Sweet Lord! unto my foolish thought
    What whisper hath replied—
"If gold or lead thy bands shall be
    'Tis I that must decide?"
The chain of gold is in Thy hand,—
    And in Thy hand for me,
When I shall bless my pain, because
    It seemeth good to Thee.

But while I murmur with my lips,
   And cloud my troubled brow,
As though I could have ruled the world
   A better way than Thou;
Forgetting, as I count my own,
   The tears which Thou hast shed,
What wonder if my fetters seem
   To weigh me down like lead!

DESOLATION.

Oh! blest are they who weep all day,
   While song and jest go by them;
Who watch by night, or wake to fight
   With demon tempters nigh them.

If they could know how blest their woe,
   With such good will they'd choose it,
In their embrace 'twould change its face,
   And they would quickly lose it.

The iron band in sorrow's hand
   Doth blind as well as bind us,
Till faith alone can make us own
   That light e'en there can find us:

Yet in that death of all but faith,
   The soul doth sow benighted
The seeds that rise, 'neath springtide skies,
   To life and bloom delighted.

THE ANGEL GUIDE.

O dearest of Angels! how sweet 'tis to know
God's Angel is with me, wherever I go;

Alone is a word without terrors for me,
For bereft of your presence I never can be.

Could you tell but a little of all you must know,
How wise about Heaven I should suddenly grow!
Yet better by far, that you hide what you see,
For thus faith will more perfectly triumph in me.

Oh! if a bright Angel with sorrow could bide,
How often my sins must have saddened my guide!
Or if a wise Angel could uselessly long,
How you must have yearned to keep me from wrong!

Were one friend upon earth as devoted as you,
Would I ever forget to be thoughtful and true?
And is it because my dull eyes cannot see,
That my heart shall not know who is walking with me?

Beautiful Angel! forgive me the past,
And help me to love and obey you at last,
And to think, when I'm tempted to sadness or fear,
That God and His Angels are watching and near.

LAURELS WON.

With the blood of mental conflict,
    With the tears of human pain,
With the rending of the heart-strings,
    And the throbbing of the brain;
In the midnight's lonely vigil,
    In the daylight's weary strife,
We must win the wreath of victors,
    On the battlefield of life.

It was so from the beginning ;
    Blood and tears were in the cup
Which for man, and, oh ! for woman,
    Man and Woman offered up ;
'Twas with Blood, He paid our ransom,
    'Twas in tears she saw It flow ;
And in blood and tears for ever,
    We must sacrifice below.

Yet take unto thy spirit
    A sweet solace, in the faith,
That its pangs will soothe thy Jesus
    Through His agony and death ;
And when all thy heart is breaking
    With the helplessness of woe,
Give thy tears to comfort Mary,
    In her loneliness below.

THE ROYAL WAY OF THE CROSS.

O ROYAL Road ! made rich and good
By Mary's tears and Jesus' blood,
Where fruit and flowers grow wild about,
And hedging thorns keep robbers out.
O royal Road ! O peerless way !
Give me to keep thee night and day.

O Road, by which the Saints have trod
Beneath the opening eye of God !
O Road, where every step can bring
The subject closer to the King !
O royal Road ! O peerless way !
Give me to keep thee night and day.

O Road, where virgins weave their crown,
Where martyrs' blood runs trickling down,

Where friendly shadows sport and play,
Lest eyes too feeble tempt the ray!
O royal Road! O peerless way!
Give me to keep thee night and day.

O Road, which broadening ere the close,
But narrow at the entrance shows;
Where Angel voices sound again,
And God goes out in search of men!
O royal Road! O peerless way!
Give me to keep thee night and day.

O road, whose fair and widening track
Stays all desire of turning back,
Whose opening views such glory shed,
That bleeding feet in gladness tread!
O royal Road! O peerless way!
Give me to keep thee night and day.

O Road, whose charms I hope to sing
In Heaven, before my Lord the King!
Through roughening pass and heightening steep,
Right joyful footing may I keep—
Till in that Heaven secure, I see
What wandering natures owe to thee,
And with exulting gladness say—
Thou royal Road! thou peerless way!

SAINT ALEXIUS.

Saint Alexius, moved by a powerful inspiration of grace, lived as a poor, unknown pilgrim in his noble father's house for the space of seventeen years. (Died 404.)

No martyr's death more sharp appears
    Than doth thy daily life,
With all its wealth of secret tears,
    And silent, secret strife:

Thy cup of joy from lip and hand
    Was flung untasted down,
For thou, on native hearth and land,
    Didst live and die alone.

Swift lost to sight in bridal hour,
    But shrined in every heart;
Thy bride still dwelt in maiden bower,
    Unwedded and apart;
Thy parents wept, a whole life through,
    The son they might not find,
And human love was strangely true
    To what it could not bind.

But thou, when years had changed thy face,
    And penance marked thy brow,
Didst seek again thy natal place,
    A nameless outcast now;
And, braver far than when a boy,
    More ripe for heavenly gain,
Didst calmly face the sight of joy,
    In close embrace of pain.

Thy father's servants still to thee
    Gave alms in daily bread,—
Bride, father, mother, thou didst see
    Pass by thy lowly shed,
And spake no word, and made no sign,
    But let earth's joys go by,
To fix each hope and aim of thine
    On joys that never die.

Oh! by thy vow so nobly kept,
    Thy crown so bravely won,
The secret tears which thou hast wept,
    The work which thou hast done,

The light about thy throne to-day,
   The rich, unmeasured store
Of endless bliss, that comes to pay
   For sorrows felt no more:

Thy hands to our great Father lift
   From thy eternal place,
To draw on us His peerless gift—
   Fidelity to Grace;—
To hear His voice, distinct and sure,
   And what that voice shall say,
With fearless faith and purpose pure,
   Unflinchingly obey:

To hear it with a dauntless will
   The world hath never schooled,
But, oh! with humble spirit still
   By lawful guidance ruled;
And so through life to play our part
   As God shall still decree,
With that unchanging aim and heart,
   Will make us like to thee.

A CURE FOR SADNESS.

How shall we climb the mountain whose summit is so steep?
How shall we clasp the counsels so difficult to keep?
How shall we train the spirit the flesh to trample down?
How shall we front the battle?—By thinking of the Crown!

If God is still the Author of life and sunshine here,
Will Heaven be such a phantom as some appear to fear?
Did God reserve but shadows of unsubstantial good
For Jesus at the pillar, and Mary by the rood?

The more the Saints have sorrowed, the ruder was
    their track,—
The greater sign that God can give wherewith to
    pay them back :
Quite sure about His Heaven, He never fears that
    they
Will chafe about their losses, or ask, "Will He repay?"

Be valiant, then, and fear not whatever shall befall!
Our war-cry through the battle—the Crown is over all;
The stronghold of our spirit—the promise of the
    Lord—
That we shall never suffer what He will not reward

MY HOLY BEADS AND MEDALS BLEST.

O GOD! if they should take away
    My Crucifix from me,
My holy Beads and Medals blest,
    How lonesome I should be!
My cherished pictures on the wall
    That meet me every day,
And smile, with such a quiet light,
    Above me when I pray.

I hang the pictures I love best
    Within my silent room,
To fill my soul with saintly joys
    And hopes beyond the tomb:

Bright angels holding crowns above,
   And dying saints below
Invite my heart to dreams of Heaven,
   And make me long to go.

I fret not for the faulty sketch,
   Nor for the carving rude,
I only seek the meanings true
   Which draw me on to good:
The Crucifix upon the wall,
   If e'er so rudely wrought,
Hath power to curb the haughty soul
   And still the angry thought.

And closest to my heart and eyes,
   "The Virgin and the Child"
Is like a well of holy thoughts
   And feelings undefiled:
I lose all taste of earthly joy,
   Before that meek embrace,
I seem to catch a glimpse of Heaven
   In Mary's virgin face.

The saints whose thoughts have charmed me most
   And cheered my onward road,
Who still direct my course from Heaven
   And light my heart for God;
Till I can kiss their footsteps there,
   I'll always joy to kneel
Before their pictured likeness here,
   And tell them all I feel.

My holy Beads and Medals blest
   At every hour I seek,
For still, before their sacred touch,
   Temptation's power is weak;

And oft I bless the God who gave
  Such strength to things so small,
That, when I hold them in my hand,
  No terror can appal.

O God! if they should take away
  My Crucifix from me,
My holy Beads and Medals blest,
  How lonesome I should be!
O God! how every day and hour,
  I cling more lovingly
Round that dear Church which hath such
    power
  To guard our hearts for Thee!

BALLAD SONGS FOR THE PEOPLE.

My spirit in the ballad song
  Doth wondrously delight,
And still, with all my practising,
  How faultily I write!
While heights of song I never reach
  Are always in my view,
To keep me quite dissatisfied
  With everything I do.

But here I'll give my notions of
  What "Ballad Songs" should be,
That others may begin the work
  Impossible to me;
For feeble words have often bid
  A great design to grow,
And whereso'er it fructify,
  'Tis well the seed to sow.

Now first—they should be picture-like,
   With groupings free and bright,
Whose attitude and colouring
   An artist would delight;
And next—they should be musical,
   With melody so gay
The children and the peasantry
   Would hum them on their way.

Familiar phrase and idiom, which
   Run wild the land about,
In choruses and burden-lines,
   Should readily rush out;
For homelily and heartily
   Must ballad-music preach
The morals that ascetic books
   So mystically teach.

Such love should overflow in them,
   That saints before the shrine
Might hear their hearts re-echoing
   In every bounding line;
And all in sound theology—
   That Rome might never need
To censure, or to pause upon
   Their version of the "Creed."

Oh! how the dream is haunting me,
   In glowing verse to write
How pleasure may be conquered by
   The fulness of delight!
To teach the poor, degraded art,
   In earthly fetters bound,
Again her own celestial harp
   Right joyfully to sound!

ANGELS AND BIRDS.

As angels praise His Name above,
   And little birds below,
I too would make the note of love
   For Him who bids it flow.
O gift! which by my God was given,
   To God you must belong,
And till I sing of love in Heaven
   I'll love on earth in song.

Oh, angels dear! that bless His name,
   Teach me to bless It too,
Oh, little birds! that sing the same
   As if His Will you knew;
This very hour I shall begin,
   By prayer and praise, to move
Towards Him who taught us both to sing,
   But only me to love.

FEAST OF THE TRANSFIGURATION.

O Lord! it is the Festival
   Of coward hearts like mine,
Who love the flowers about the cross,
   The light upon the shrine,
And, when in sight of Calvary,
   Are comforted to know
That Thabor was Thy resting-place
   A little while below.

The light was on Thy raiment then,
   The halo round Thy Face,
And yet Thou wast as truly there,
   In glory and in grace,
As when upon the hill of woe
   The streaming Life-Blood ran,
Till nature was convulsed to see
   How God could die for man.

But, Lord! they do not always flee
   From Thy dark hour of pain,
Who gladly in the sunny light
   Of thy sweet smile remain;
Saint John beneath the gory cross
   Was all more fond and true,
Because he could remember there
   What Thabor gave to view.

To Mary's peerless heart alone
   Thou didst not need to show
The brightness of Thy Majesty,
   To bind her to Thy woe:
Still, souls not half so weak as mine,
   On this world's gloomy way,
Will smile to meet a Festival
   Which gladdens like to-day.

MOTHER OF MERCY.

'Twas for the sake of sinners
   That thou wast formed so pure;
If we had ne'er been wounded,
   Thou ne'er hadst come to cure:

'Tis by our human weakness
  Thy royal power doth live:
Thou art the Queen of Mercy,
  To pity and forgive.

'Tis thy perpetual pleading,
  Thy mother-cry above
Which thrills, in sweetest music,
  To God's own heart of love;
It stays His arm uplifted,
  Till, from His royal throne,
He seems to bless the mercy
  Which justifies His own.

Go, think upon her sorrows,
  Then wonder, if you will,
That God hath made her glories
  A greater marvel still;
That He who pays in Heaven
  One thought of Him on earth,
Hath blessed a Mother's fondness,
  And crowned a Mother's worth

THE LEGEND OF BLESSED IMELDA LAMBERTINI,

WHO DIED THROUGH JOY AND LOVE ON MAKING HER FIRST COMMUNION, 1335.

IMELDA LAMBERTINI is the Saint of whom I tell,
She lived pure 'mid pomp and splendour, as a nun within her cell;
But her childish heart was carried with such zeal to things divine,
That she prayed to quit the palace and draw closer to the shrine.

So they bore her to a convent, where the Sisters held
 the rule
Of our holy Father Dominic, for her cradle and her
 school;
And the nuns who saw her spirit, did she work or
 did she pray,
Dropped the seed of pious teaching in her young heart
 day by day.

Imelda Lambertini loved each nun that she drew
 nigh,
And her brow bent low and lower for the habit
 passing by;
And each word of holy counsel fell like music on her
 ear,
And, within her heart upspringing, made its goodly
 fruit appear.

But Imelda Lambertini had a Teacher in the
 shrine,
Where the Hidden God imbued her with a sense of
 things divine;
And when all her young companions were at play
 upon the sward,
Came Imelda to the altar, and knelt down before her
 Lord.

So they twined about her spirit, so they grew into her
 soul,
The high secrets of the altar that they swelled beyond
 control;
And she prayed, with her warm pleadings, that her
 heart might be the shrine
Of the Hidden God who bathed her in His tenderness
 divine.

But the nuns who heard her pleadings and had pity on her tears,
While they blessed her ardent longings, yet repelled her infant years;
And the holy child Imelda made no answer, said no word,
But went back again all weeping and knelt down before her Lord.

How the yearnings rose within her for the glory and the bliss,
How her heart beat strong and stronger with the longing to be His!
Till the prayer of her young being, in its passionate request,
Was a loud cry to the Saviour who awoke it in her breast.

The Host hath left the altar, and, with circling rays around,
It shines bright above Imelda where she kneeleth on the ground;
And the nuns, who see the wonder, bring the priest unto her side,
And the priest saith, " Now, Imelda may no longer be denied."

So, she feeds upon the banquet she hath longed for up to this,
And they leave her to her praying, and they leave her to her bliss,—
And when once again they seek her, there's an awe upon the place,
For so close she clasped her Saviour, that she died in His embrace.

A PARENT'S PRAYER.

Have pity on their youth, dear God!
    Have pity on their age;
May'st Thou their lives' best thoughts employ,
    Their hearts' first love engage;
Beginning with the many—well,
    But ending like the few,
And safe from those disturbing joys
    Which hide Thee from their view.

Oh! lead them by the hand, dear God!
    And guide and guard their way,
Ere yet the world hath found a lure
    To turn their steps astray;
So pour Thy love around them now,
    That they shall never bear,
In after-life, a joy to know
    Thou dost refuse to share.

Oh! go before their steps, dear God!
    And warn them how to flee
From sin, before they hear its voice,
    Or turn their eyes to see,
E'en like that fair and royal Saint,
    Who (Saxon legends show)
Could scarce be said to leave the world
    She did not ever know.

'Tis sweet before Thy Shrine to kneel,
    In humble hope of Heaven,
Because to her who loved so much,
    So much was once forgiven;

But what the Saviour can forgive,
    The sinner can't forget,
And where the sin returns no more,
    The sorrow lingers yet.

So still I say, preserve them, God!
    And to the young I tell,
The mercy that forgives the sin
    Can hinder it as well;
And he who never leaves his God
    Is spared the bitter woe
Of having pierced the One kind Heart
    That broke for him below.

THE TREASURE OF LOVE.

"IN CRUCE SALUS."

I can see through the darkness the tracery dim
Of the cross that leads onward my spirit to Him,
And I think, in His anguish, how darkly He died—
So pierced for my pleasure, so mocked for my pride.

Oh! sweet 'twere to suffer all night and all day,
To smooth for one moment the bed where He lay,
To lighten by pity the sorrows I shared,
And to sicken and languish that He might be spared.

Then, merciful Jesus, what thanks should I give,
Who still in such anguish am destined to live,
That every new hour, I can offer to Thee
Salt tears for the Life-Blood so lavished on me!

DEWDROPS ON THORNS.

Is there nothing wondrous
   In a love so true,
That it brought a mighty God
   Down to die for you?
Is there nothing glorious
   In the thought so bright,
That He upon the royal throne
   Will place you at His right?

Is there nothing hopeful
   In each sight and sound
Of His watchful kindness,
   All our lives around?—
Springing joys that cheer us,
   Tears that keep us true,
Hopes that when we're drooping
   Lift us up anew.

O my God! my Glory!
   How can I repine,
While to glad and cheer me
   Such fair wonders shine?—
Light for my assurance,
   Shadows for my gain,—
Since all human merit
   Springs from human pain.

LOVE'S TRIALS.

*"Thou turnedst away Thy face from me, and I became troubled."—
Ps. xxix, 8.*

My Lord! the happy days are past
  When Thou wast all to me,
When, like a star within my breast,
  Shone the full thought of Thee:
When prayer lay like a quiet song,
  Upon my lips all day,
And Angels seemed to walk with me,
  And smile upon my way.

My Lord! how often have I knelt
  Before Thy shrine in prayer,
And never passed beyond the thought
  That God, my God, was there;
While still, in speechless wonder, all
  The hours went gliding by,
And left me where they found me first—
  For God, my God, was nigh.

My Lord! with what a lonesome pain
  I kneel before Thee now,
And strive to check a wandering eye,
  And calm a troubled brow,
And say to vague, distracting thoughts—
  "I know my God is there,"—
Yet know it with too dead a faith
  For tenderness or prayer.

A thousand times I ask my soul
  If all Thy love is o'er,
A thousand times I cry to Thee
  For one assurance more;

I look within, I look without—
   I know not where Thou art,
But Thou hast left a fearful void
   In Thy poor creature's heart.

I seem to court reproof, because
   If I could see the wrong,
I then might chase it from my heart,
   And still to Thee belong;
But wearily, so wearily
   My sluggish life goes by,
And still, its outward seeming is
   The same to every eye.

At times, to quiet my sick heart,
   I tell her Thou art blest,
That Thou can'st never know the pangs
   Which rend this aching breast;
That Thou, who art far more myself
   Than I can ever be,
Art God in Thy eternal right,
   Whate'er becomes of me.

At times, to look upon Thy cross
   Rebukes my wild despair,
For surely 'twas no changeling's love
   Which lived and triumphed *there;*
And, clasping Thy dear Feet, I say,
   "Turn as Thou wilt from me,
The soul Thy dying cry hath bought
   Will never turn from Thee."

Oh! take me to Thy bleeding Heart,
   And hide me fondly there,
Send down Thy light upon my thought,
   Thy peace into my prayer;

Or grant me yet the noblest boon
  Around me or above—
To clasp Thy cross, to share Thy fate,
  To suffer and to love.

SHIFTING SCENES.

ALL my day is dark and lonely,
Dark as night itself could prove;
I can do no work, but only
Singing to Thine ear of love:
Through my soul the hope was springing
That my life might henceforth be
Acting songs, instead of singing,
Braving every ill for Thee.

Thou hast seen the hope and stilled it;
Now my heart beats faint and weak,
Many a weary pain hath chilled it
Since such yearnings dared to speak:
Midnight gloom kept gathering round me,
Hope and joy refused to soar,
Till at last strange terrors bound me
To my prison-room once more.

Is my sole vocation—singing?
Praying when my pain is strong,
And from each new anguish wringing
Fire to light another song.
Ah! my Love, if thus I borrow
Music welcome to Thine ear,
Give my soul enough of sorrow
To be still Thy minstrel here.

When 'twas once my loved vocation
Touching harp-strings all the day,
Thou did'st check the inspiration,
And forbid the chords to play;
Now that harp is set before me
Which Thyself hast hid so long,
And my noontide hours adore Thee
Only in a dreamy song.

Touch my lips for this sweet singing,
Since 'tis all they must impart;
Send the life-tides warmer springing
Through the fountains of my heart;
Bathe my soul in hues of glory
Caught from many a saintly shrine,
Till I preach, in song and story,
For this peerless Church of Thine.

OUR HOLY MOTHER THE CHURCH

Sing! for the Spouse victorious,
  Throned in her Home divine,
Crown'd with the wreath so glorious
  None but a God can twine:
Look to the joys that greet her,
  Leap to her heart of love:
Oh! what bright bliss to meet her
  In her own land above!

Strike! for the Spouse all bleeding,
  Dauntless 'mid deadliest strife,
Foe after foe succeeding
  Smites at the world's best life.

Trust to the smile so fearless,
   True to its Godlike birth;
Strike for the brave and peerless,
   The militant Church on earth!

Wail! for the poor Spouse weeping
   Far from her queenly throne,
Sadly the night-watch keeping
   Down in her dungeon lone.
Ah! through her pain and sorrow
   Best may your love be seen :
Pray, since your prayers can borrow
   Aid for the crownless Queen.

ASPIRATION.

ENLIGHTEN me to know Your will
   And strengthen me to do it;
Prepare my heart to meet Your love
   And cling for ever to it.

REMEMBER ME.

THINK what a world He spread for you!
   How kindly and how fair
The summer light, the summer bloom
   That He has lavished there;
While still on every glancing wave
   And every leafy tree
His mighty finger writes the word—
        Remember me!

Think what a bright and royal scene
  His love hath caused to bloom
Around your very prison-house
  Of trial and of gloom;
And, when you clasp the smiling flowers
  Or watch the gliding wave
Remember still, in all your joy,
      To think who gave.

Oh! had His word been—to forget,
  Who could have then obeyed?
Forget the Heart that loves us most!
  Forget the Hand that made!
Fain would I choose the better part,
  From earth and air and sea
Still turning, to forget Thy works
      And think of Thee.

TO ST. ALPHONSUS

ON MY TWENTY-SIXTH BIRTHDAY.

My faithful Saint Alphonsus,
  No birthday ever brought
To me before such yearning hopes
  Or high, ambitious thought;
For though from earliest infancy
  In virtue's path you trod,
At twenty-six, you often say,
  Began your life for God.

And thus, at twenty-six, I know,
  Began the struggling years
Of conflict between grace divine
  And human hopes and fears;

For nature held her smaller share,
   A subject in your soul,
But burst in fierce rebellion forth
   When grace would have the whole.

How often do I sit and think
   Upon that "three days' war,"
When, locked within your chamber fast,
   You kept the world afar,
Because the strife was hard enough
   With maddening heart and brain
And demon whispers tempting back
   To that false world again.

How often do I seem to hang
   My fate upon your own,
And ask you, in my trembling soul,
   To live for God alone;
For every light seemed quenched for me
   And every hope seemed fled,
When, speaking through your look again,
   You raised me from the dead.

Oh! had you missed your special crown,
   E'en though your soul had past
To peace in Heaven's secure abodes—
   Where would mine own be cast?
Who knows if grace, so sadly lost,
   Had e'er been found again,
If your free heart consented not
   To God's low whisper then.

And ever, as these thoughts arise,
   How yearningly I crave
To be myself another saint,
   Some wandering soul to save;

Till had I but this aim alone,
    I fain would choose the best,
In hope that through my prayers at last
    Another might be blest.

O Saint Alphonsus! won't you bless
    My rising hopes to-day,
And help me more than ever now
    To find the "one strait way;"
And finding, still to keep so well
    That I, with you, may say
My soul began to live for God,
    Her twenty-sixth birthday.

THE OUTLAW.

Yes, I have outlawed *self* to-day,
    And though I could not kill,
There's no one but is free to slay
    The traitor at his will:
On every count he has been tried,
    And guilty found in all;
And never more I'll take his side—
    His case, unheard, must fall.

From this day forth no friendly part
    Let *self* expect from me;
Whoever drives him from my heart
    My chosen friend shall be;
And if he still refuse to die
    In battle-press and shout,
I am at last resolved to try
    If I can starve him out.

I never yet have sat me down,
   The case of *self* to read,
But I have felt my spirit groan
   Above each lawless deed:
I never yet have fixed an hour
   To hear the traitor sue,
But judgment lost her rightful power
   And failed her work to do.

Then never more a friendly part
   Let *self* expect from me;
Whoever drives him from my heart
   My chosen friend shall be;
And, though he haunt me day and night
   An audience to implore,
I am at last determined quite
   To hear his case no more.

VERSES FOR EVERY HOUR IN THE DAY.

ONE O'CLOCK.

THE clock strikes One!—oh, number dread!
   Which still repeats to me
One God in Heaven, One Soul on earth,
   And One Eternity.

One God who sees and judges all,
   One Soul in danger still,
And One Eternity, heaped up
   With boundless good or ill.

One God—with all my masters, then,
   I have but One to please;
One Soul—and shall I risk or lose,
   This dying flesh to ease?

And One Eternity;—my soul,
   Through Christ's sweet Blood implore,
That He would save thee, who—if lost,
   Art lost for evermore!

TWO O'CLOCK.

The clock strikes Two!—oh, gracious hour!
   Whose chiming tones are fraught
With the rich work of love and power
   Which God Incarnate wrought.

Divine and Human, once apart,
   Are fused so fondly now
That God has loved with human heart,
   Since Jesus lived below.

Again, my favourite hour displays
   Another charm whene'er
I think how Jesus fixed His gaze
   On one sweet Handmaid fair—

To drink from his unsweetened cup,
   To mingle tears with gore,
And, in her pierced heart, offer up
   The wounds His Body bore.

For, since our woe was doubly wrought,
   It lifts our hopes anew
To see such full salvation brought
   By Man and Woman too.

THREE O'CLOCK.

The clock strikes Three!—this mystic hour
   Invites my soul to pray
To Him whose Wisdom, Love, and Power
   Are round me night and day.

Oh! had I weighed this thought alone—
   That God is still with me,
What evil dare my soul have done
   Before the Sacred Three?

His Wisdom all my secrets knew,
   His Power alone held back
For the dear Love that ever drew
   His mercy on my track.

O Sacred Trinity on high!
   Before Thee now I fall,
In tears for every hour gone by,
   While Thou wast not my All.

FOUR O'CLOCK.

The clock strikes Four!—My soul, beware,
   This hour is full for thee—
The "Four last things" are hinted there;
   Think what these things may be.

Death, with his aspect stern and rude,
   Just Judgment's fixed award,
And Hell or Heaven, as bad or good,
   The servant meets his Lord.

O Christ! whose death must sweeten mine,
   Still grant my life to prove,
At shadowy distance, like to Thine,
   In patience and in love.

FIVE O'CLOCK.

The clock strikes Five!—this saving hour
    Invites my soul to take
Her refuge in the Wounds which bled
    So freely for her sake.

The piercèd Feet—the tortured Hands—
    The Heart laid bare for me!
O dying Love! O bleeding Love!
    May I, too, die for Thee.

The dying life is all I crave
    Which dies to self each day;
The loving death which bears the soul
    To her true life away!

SIX O'CLOCK.

The clock strikes Six!—though Precepts few
    Doth holy Church unroll,
I will respect her counsels too
    And keep them in my soul:—

I'll seek her spirit through her laws,
    While in her ranks I stand,
Nor ever wound her heart because
    No rod is in her hand.

Let others watch her words through fear,
    I'll work her will for love,
Content to fight her battles here
    And wait her smiles above.

SEVEN O'CLOCK.

The clock strikes Seven!—Oh! think awhile
   What sevenfold grief is here;
And, would you bask in Mary's smile,
   Be kind to Mary's tear.

Mourn for the heart that pined so long,
   The eyes that wept so much;
And, if unmoved at Jesus' wrong,
   Let Mary's sorrow touch.

'Tis said, the hearts so stern and cold
   That doomed the Son to die,
Were strangely softened to behold
   The Mother standing by.

EIGHT O'CLOCK.

The clock strikes Eight!—her strokes recall
   Eight states which Christ hath blest;
Now search, my soul, among them all
   Where may'st thou find thy rest.

Ah, Lord! how sad, if I should prove
   My thoughts so far from Thee
That many a mild award of love
   Found thankless heart in me.

Teach me to think as Thou hast thought,
   To see as Thou dost see,
Nor ever turn away from aught
   Which hath been blessed by Thee.

NINE O'CLOCK.

The clock strikes Nine!—Oh, joyous hour!
   Nine choirs of Angels raise
Exulting hymns, with all their power,
   To their Creator's praise;

And, while my earthly work I do,
   They teach my soul to share
In their unbroken worship too
   And never-ending prayer:

For prayer and praise are sweetly wrought
   Through every night and day,
In which God's will is simply sought,
   And self-will cast away.

TEN O'CLOCK.

The clock strikes Ten!—ten lepers sought
   Their cure in sore distress;
Yet, when the kindly cure was wrought,
   But *one* came back to bless:

The nine went hurrying on their track,
   Old friends once more to see,
The Tenth, a stranger, turned him back,
   He had no friend but Thee.

Lord, to whose hands my life I owe,
   Still grant my soul to be
The pilgrim stranger here below,
   For all sweet service free.

ELEVEN O'CLOCK.

Eleven o'clock!—the number calls
  With warning voice to me
Who came in the "Eleventh hour,"
  An idler, Lord, to Thee.

But still the kindly parable
  Doth my slow soul invite,
Since I have come, the last of all,
  To work with all my might;

And strive, with right good will, to pay
  The long arrears I owe,
By working for no hire but what
  Thou deignest to bestow.

TWELVE O'CLOCK.

The clock strikes Twelve!—Twelve fishers rude,
  Of humble speech and birth,
Did Christ send forth to preach His Word
  And plant His Church on earth;

For God works not by human ways
  Nor bends to human doubt,
And rarely do His means seem fit
  To bring His ends about:

But simple heart and ceaseless prayer,
  With will prepared to do,
May bring us yet to serve His Church
  As Saints and Martyrs too.

LIGHT ON THE HILL-TOP.

Sing away, sing away, by night or by day,
This world is a world which is passing away;
Be its highways or by-ways as rough as they please,
They are leading to regions of sunshine and ease.

The steeper the hill is, the grander the height,
And the higher the summit, the prospect more bright;
Then, upwards and onwards, no pause on the road,
Till we rest from our toils at the feet of our God.

MOUNT THABOR.

My soul is bright, as if the light
   From that far mountain streaming
Came o'er to-day, in many a ray,
   Upon my spirit beaming.

I hear no sound of joy around
   And pain is spread before me,
But still that light from Thabor's height
   Keeps shining strangely o'er me.

What can it be, so new to me
   Whose way through darkness lying,
Doth rarely find a ray so kind
   To shed its light undying?

It thrills my thought, as if it brought
    Assurance full before me.
With Calv'ry's band I soon must stand
    And see the dread Cross o'er me;

But He whose ray shines bright to-day,
    Will then, as sure be nigh me,
To bear me through the anguish too,
    If He be pleas'd to try me.

And while I weep, if I but keep
    His shield of prayer around me,
The Cross will be such strength to me,
    I'll bless the day it found me.

So, sing the light on Thabor's height
    While yet it cheers our sadness;
And should it leave, oh! then receive
    The Cross with equal gladness;

And sing all day the self-same way,
    Or raise the strain still higher,
On fire to prove our Bleeding Love
    Is all our hearts' desire;

On fire to show, through weal or woe,
    His ways can still delight us;
That should He like to pierce or strike
    We'll bless the Hands that smite us,

And hold our faith through life and death;
    His Love is still our Master,
And only strays through lonely ways
    That ours may cling the faster.

Oh, Jesus dear! our portion here,
  Our only All hereafter,
While Thy whole life was tears and strife,
  Shall ours be song and laughter?

SWANLIKE.

Be like the noble bird that goes
  In silence down the wave
And never sings until she knows
  She's hastening to her grave:
Thus, calm and watchful, glide along
  Through Life's delusive tide,
And wisely keep thy triumph-song
  Till Death is at thy side.

HARBOUR THE HARBOURLESS.

My Lord! dost Thou teach me such words to apply
To Thee, the Creator of earth and of sky,
To Thee, the great Monarch whom angels attend,
Existing for ever, and never to end?

Yes, "harbour the harbourless" still dost Thou say,
And see! I have opened my heart to obey,
And pray Thee, poor Pilgrim! to take Thy repose
While I work for Thy service and weep for Thy woes.

Alas! when I see Thee all bleeding and bare,
With nothing to comfort and no one to care,
Forgot in Thy temples, despised in Thy poor,—
Thy need of a harbour seems bitter and sure.

Then teach me henceforward Thy word to obey,
To "harbour the harbourless" day after day,
To deck out thy dwelling with cost and with care,
To cleanse it in penance and gild it in prayer.

THE ANGEL-KEEPERS.

Angels of the altar! who
   Keep a watch undying,
A sleepless vigil ever true
   Where my Lord is lying,
Long ago when forced to part,
   All in bitter weeping,
I resigned my trembling heart
   To your holy keeping.

In your charge I bid it stay,
   Lest the world should sever
From the vows I pledged that day,
   And hold it captive ever:
You I prayed to fill the cup
   From your burning treasure,
Flowing o'er and brimming up
   And loving beyond measure.

Angels of the altar! true,
   Years have since passed over,
Sleepless watchers still are you
   Round a sleepless Lover:
My poor heart as ever lives
   Fainting, failing, weeping
Very little sign it gives
   Of angelic keeping!

GOD IN ALL.

Since Thou canst smile with many a ray
    And thrill with many a tone,
Oh! wherefore should I watch all day
    For *one* delight alone?
Thy sunshine now may glad my heart,
    And then Thy stars may rise,
'Tis always Thou who dost impart
    Their grandeurs to the skies.

So grant me, God, Thine every gift
    To sing with homage free,
And still may every rapture lift
    My spirit up to Thee;
For many a star will rise and fall
    And many a beam will stray,
But Thou, who art the Lord of all,
    Wilt never turn away.

TO THE HEART OF SAINT PHILIP NERI.

O heart! whose ceaseless beatings still
    Were all for God alone,
Which sent, with each mysterious thrill,
    A love-sigh to his own,
Which glowed like any sun within,
    Consuming life away;
Some share of thy warm radiance fling
    On my cold heart to-day.

O heart! which with such burning zeal
    Embraced the cross in all,
For very joy thou couldst not feel
    Its pain or weight at all;
But cried, in saintly patience strong,
    " 'Tis Paradise below!"
Teach me to chant the triumph-song
    Which Christ's true martyrs know.

"TASTE AND SEE."

LITTLE they care to shut their ears
    To life's unmeaning sound
Who hear the music of the spheres
    In their own souls resound.

Little they care to close their eyes
    To curious show and sight
Who see the forms of angels rise
    To cheer them through the night.

All types of glad and glorious things
    Are through the senses given,
That thus the soul may plume her wings
    And turn her flight to Heaven.

But, oh! what wondrous sights they lose,
    What rapturous sounds they miss
Who taste earth's joy, and then refuse
    To seek a purer bliss!

Little they think, when angels sing
  And bright-robed saints appear,
Of the few drops of joy that spring
  To our bleak exile here!

Little they'll laugh in after-days
  Who wandering lights pursue,
When Heaven, with all its countless rays,
  Will ne'er delight their view.

THE VALIANT WOMAN.

"Mulierem fortem quis inveniet?"—*Prov.* xxxi.

A MOTHERLY and gracious thing—
  True woman, in whatever class,
Whose looks, from very kindness, fling
  A loving shadow as they pass.

With swift steps gliding to and fro,
  But ever lingering wheresoe'er
The helpless wail of woman's woe,
  Or groan of manhood meets her ear.

By loathsome sickness still she stands,
  Or, if the need should be,
She serves—but with such willing hands
  As shows the service free.

Young children cling about her feet,
  Rude boys will cease their play,
Attracted by her spirit sweet,
  And, for mere love, obey.

The mourner needs her soothing word,
　　She hides the sinner's shame,
While young and old, with one accord,
　　Breathe blessings on her name.

Of duties manifold, not one
　　Is slighted, but above
And round them evermore is hung
　　An atmosphere of love.

No action but is lit by thought,
　　No thought but leads to where
Some righteous action may be wrought,
　　And steeped in hidden prayer.

The death-bed finds her kneeling by,
　　An influence and power,
With heart that ever yearns to die
　　In God's appointed hour.

Her ordered household, all in tone
　　Like some harmonious lay,
Go forth upon the pathway shown,
　　Scarce feeling they obey.

The spirit with such noiseless tread
　　Glides through them everywhere,
Scarce knowing by what impulse led,
　　They live and labour there.

But who hath fully understood
　　What secret power is won
Where joy means only doing good,
　　Or knowing good is done?

EVERYTHING FOR THEE.

I HAVE a thousand things to say,
   A thousand works I see,
A thousand things to think about,
   And everything for Thee!
I have to say my prayers at night,
   And when I wake, again,
It may be all the day besides,
   Though more in whispers then;
To speak a word of counsel here,
   A word of pity there,
To give a warning kindly meant
   Falls often to my share.
I can have gay thoughts for the young,
   To show that Faith is bliss,
I can have patience with the old
   Till they, too, think of this;
I can have beatings in my heart
   And plottings in my brain,
And pleasant rhymes and sunny thoughts
   And *all* that Thou mayst reign!
My stories by the winter fire,
   My walks on flow'ry sod,
My smile at jest or praise of tune,
   Are all for Thee, my God!
My share of good, the whole day long,
   Is finished e'en by me
Thus trying to forget myself
   And everything but Thee!

DEFENCE.

"Every man's sword upon his thigh because of fears in the night."—Cant. iii.

Around the bed of Solomon, the couch of sweet repose,
Why is it, Lord, in armour all these mailèd warriors
 close?
"Because of fears," Thy answer is, "of sudden fears
 by night,
The clash of arms may break their sleep, when they
 must wake to fight."

And, Lord, when I am peacefully reposing thus with
 Thee,
Can foes arise in sudden swarm to mock and menace
 me?
"Yes, child," methinks I hear Thee say, "without
 the shield of prayer
Thou art not safe in slumber here; so gird thee and
 prepare.

"In pity to thy feebleness I rest thy soul to-night,
But none can tell the day or hour when thou must
 wake to fight;
Then never lay thy arms aside; rest on, but resting
 know
The chamber of King Solomon is open to the foe."

TAKING SANCTUARY.

I smile into Thy face, my God!
 When most it frowns on me,
Because I know my helplessness
 Is crying out to Thee:

I have no other help on earth
  If Thou shouldst leave me here,
And thus I am so sure of Thee
  That nothing makes me fear.

It is not that my foes have ceased
  To threaten and to storm,
It is not that my sins appear
  In less repulsive form,
It is not that Thy saving voice
  Has bid my terrors fly—
Ah! no, for very helplessness,
  My hope shoots up so high.

'Twould not be like a Godlike God,
  A true, Almighty King,
To let Thy potent arrows fly
  At such a feeble thing!
And well I know none else can harm,
  While Thou art by to see
The trembling culprit who has fled
  For Sanctuary to Thee.

THE VISION OF SAINT AGNES OF MONTE-PULCIANO, VIRGIN OF THE ORDER OF SAINT DOMINIC.

Saint Agnes, in vision, seemed to weep upon the shore,
A stormy sea before her and no bark to take her o'er,
When three stately ships appearing, proffered peace unto her thought,
For she saw that each could bear her to the haven that she sought.

A form of saintly bearing from each deck appeared to rise,
She knew that Saint Augustine was the closest to her eyes,
But Saint Dominic and Saint Francis seemed on either hand to be,
With a smile that fell, like moonlight, o'er that desolating sea.

Then, each began in turn to invite her to pass o'er,
In his ship of gallant building, from her exile on the shore,
Recounting all the pilgrims he had guided to their goal,
Till election seemed to fail her, and she wavered in her soul.

When Saint Dominic saw her pausing, he held out his hand to aid,
And the spell that instant breaking, left her wond'ring and afraid;
But she never after doubted *whose* the gallant bark should be
That would bear her, calm and smiling, o'er the horrors of the sea.

MARY AND MARTHA.

Mary, at the Saviour's Feet,
Bowed in meekness ever,
From her calm and loved retreat
Has no thought to sever:

Neither does she care to ask
    Why her restless neighbour
Seeks not near the Sun to bask,
    Turning all to labour.

Martha is not so resigned
    To her sister's choice,
At the Saviour's Feet reclined,
    Listening to His voice.
Little Martha heeds or knows
    How their duties vary!
Quickly to the Lord she goes,
    And complains of Mary.

Every age the same doth see;
    Zealous now as ever,
Martha from the Saviour's knee
    Fain would Mary sever:
Oh! let Mary bear the frown
    Of so dear a neighbour,
Till her silent prayer brings down
    Blessings on her labour.

THE TABERNACLE.

"*Lord, it is good for us to be here.*"—*Matt.* xvii. 4.

WHEN I kneel before Thee there,
    Life itself is changed for me;
I forget the very prayer
    That I came to make to Thee;
Scarcely I recall the names
    That I wanted most to say,
Losing sight of all the claims
    Men have on me when I pray.

My poor soul, so void of good,
   Meeting snares on every side,
Challenged now to combats rude,
   Then by her own weakness tried,
Through the glorious hour which gives
   God to her enraptured gaze,
In His being breathes and lives
   And rejoices more than prays.

But when I depart at last—
   Counting hours that must drag o'er
'Ere another night be past,
   And my life begin once more,—
Slow to leave a joy so sweet,
   As I linger near the porch,
How contrasts the crowded street
   With the still, deserted church!

'Tis Thy creatures onward press,
   Full of plans and thoughtless glee,
Full of business, full of dress,
   Full of everything but Thee!
Trader, there is gold above,
   That one passing prayer might win;
Woman, oh! you dream not love
   Like to that which burns within.

Bounteous God! so rich, so true,
   Quick to hear and kind to call!
For the cloister naming few,
   On the altar born for all!
One grace more—where all seem given—
   Let us *act* as if we knew
That the God who reigns in Heaven,
   Lives within our churches too.

SAINT WILFRID AND ROME.

Saint Wilfrid, Bishop of York, in the persecutions which he suffered, invariably appealed to Rome and made several journeys to that city. (Died 709.)

Like the battle's strong music, how bravely it rolled,
The life of Saint Wilfrid, the simple and bold!
So leal to his Church and so leal to his land,
And so fit for his tools as they came to his hand;
So fearless to fight and so tranquil to bear,
So easy to yield and so princely to dare;
An outcast abroad or a captive at home,
He but asks his assailants to meet him at Rome.

Oh! rude was the path which he trod by at times,
When they jeered him with folly or charged him with crimes,
When they thwarted with evil or crossed him in good,
When clients forsook him and patrons withstood;
When churches and abbeys were wrenched from his grasp,
When souls that he cherished broke loose from his clasp:
But stripped of his portion and chased from his home,
He was sure of his welcome in turning to Rome.

Oh! loathsome the air of his dungeon might be,
And weary his journeys by land and by sea;
The parting from true hearts a shadow might cast,
The falsehood of cold hearts might chill with its blast:

While snares round his pathway and kings for his foes
Make peril and danger wherever he goes;
But little he recks them, abroad or at home,
For he trusts in his stronghold—St. Peter and Rome.

He knew her* by sense, and he knew her by sight,
He lived in her beauty he cleaved to her right;
He fought out her battles again and again,
And whene'er he was worsted he cried to her then;
And whoever was graceless, whoever was cold,
Rome knew her own Champion—Wilfrid the Bold;
And she bent full of fondness to welcome him home,
When, as child to his mother, came Wilfrid to Rome.

'Twas the dream of his youth and the crown of his age,
Her spirit to win and her battle to wage;
'Twas the love of the boy and the life of the man,
And the current went deep'ning as onward it ran;
Till the breath of her air or the glow of her skies
Was health to his spirit and light to his eyes;
Till, wherever he wandered, his heart was at home
And throned like a monarch in visions of Rome.

No wonder, as life was awaiting its close,
That visions of beauty all silently rose,
That voices came floating around and above
From the land of his worship, the shrine of his love,
Which had soothed him in exile, had saved him from wrong,
Had won him so early and held him so long—
No wonder his spirit, in seeking its home,
Turned earthward a moment to gaze upon Rome.

* Rome.

No wonder our hearts, as they silently cast
Their looks full of questioning thought to the past,
Should see, in that Saint, full of labours and years,
An anchor to rest on, in hopes and in fears :
Whether building his churches or singing his psalms,
Or helping the poor with his prayers and his alms ;
A preacher abroad or a pastor at home,
How, helpful and hopeful, he leans upon Rome.

He frets not for fortunes he cannot command,
But, whatever his tools are, he takes them in hand ;
He gathers from all things what all can produce
To answer his purpose and serve for his use ;
He stands by the block, a true Martyr in will,
But crossed in his purpose, a Confessor still :
They may tear from the Bishop his flock and his home,
But the Missioner still can be working for Rome.

Oh ! lift up our hearts by the might of your own,
To tend to one centre and seek it alone ;
When clouds are above and when darts are abroad,
To hear but our conscience and fear but our God ;
To ask for no quarter if nature should fight,
To yield to no pressure when armed for the right ;
In peril at peace and in labour at home,
And, while waiting for Heaven, still working for Rome.

TO MY CREATOR.

"What have I in Heaven? and besides Thee, what do I desire upon earth?"
Ps. lxxii, 25.

I AM your *creature*, O my Lord!
How much is in that simple word!
Let sickness waste, or sorrow kill,
O Lord! I am Your creature still.

You have not bid me live in vain,
You weigh my pleasure and my pain;
I am Your own eternal thought,
And You will care for what You wrought.

I'd rather be the simplest fly,
That wakes at noon, at night to die,
Within Your love, beneath Your care,
Than own the world and You not there.

In Heaven itself there seems to be
One only resting-place for me,
For I can only wish to go
To Him who makes my heaven below.

NIGHT AND MORNING.

My God! I am longing for morning;
  It chases all slumber away,
To think about Mass and Communion,
  So soon to come on with the day!

Too slowly the minutes seem creeping,
  Which lead to Thine altar and Thee;
If night were not here by Thy bidding,
  How terribly long it would be!

My God! I am longing for morning;
  Yet fain would I rest through the night,
That so I might wake all the stronger,
  To bless Thee with morning's first light:
But still, through the shade and the silence,
  The thrill of Thy whisper divine
Is waking my spirit for ever,
  To love and be happy with Thine.

My God! I am longing for morning;
  And if I should sleep till it shine,
What hours will be wasted from loving
  The Heart which still watches o'er mine!
Yet, strengthen my body with slumber,
  That so it may labour for Thee,
But still, let me dream of my Saviour,
  Till morning shall bring Him to me.

OUR LIVING ROSARY.

How oft mine eyes have dwelt upon
  "The Virgin and the Child,"
How oft my heart hath lingered in
  A resting-place so mild!
Of all the sacred images,
  The sweetest 'twas to me—
But now, with what an altered soul,
  Its loveliness I see!

I think the Joyful Mysteries
    Are closing in my life,
Because, where'er I lift mine eyes
    To nerve me for the strife,
'Tis on the mournful crucifix
    Their gaze is wont to stay,
And, though the *God* still meets me there,
    The *Child* has passed away.

But, as the joys are all but gone,
    The sorrows, too, will fly,
And then the glories will come forth
    To brighten earth and sky;
Till, in these crowning mysteries,
    We see with glad surprise,
With regal front, no more to die,
    The ancient joys arise.

THE CRUCIFIX.

Those Blessed Wounds, all pain to Thee,
Are rest, and hope, and love to me;
That crown of thorns which shamed Thee so,
Makes all my glory here below.
But I—can I not offer yet
Small payment for so great a debt?
And clasp my pains, howe'er they rend,
As love-gifts from my kindest Friend?
And gladly suffer, while I live,
New pleasure to my God to give?

Those precious stigmas in my soul
Plant by many a grievous dole;
Let me grieve until I know
Something of my Saviour's woe;

Still increase these tears of mine
Till I learn to pity Thine;
Wring new life-drops from my heart
Till it feels of Thine the smart.

O my God, my Love, my All!
It seems to me I hear Thy call,
Bidding me to do for Thee
That which Thou hast done for me.

AN ACT OF HOMAGE.

THE lutes of the Angels are silent for me,
The smile on Thy fair face no longer I see;
My soul is all gloomy and shrinking with fear,
Her lights and her glories no longer are here.

'Tis darkness around me, and darkness within,
No warm ray of sunshine my spirit doth win;
My prayers are unanswered, my griefs are unknown,
The God that I worshipped has left me alone.

But still does my fond heart in ecstasy rise
To think that His glory still lives in the skies,
That God is eternal, all-potent, and free,
Untouched by the shadows that fall upon me.

O Spirit of glory! O Spirit of love!
Still waking to rapture around and above,
Exulting with conquest, o'erflowing with bliss,
What joy for Thy creature like thinking on *this!*

Oh, when shall my spirit be lost in Thine Own,
To live on the breath of Thy triumph alone,
To spring to Thy Heaven, exulting and free,
This *I* quenched for ever which warreth with *Thee!*

CONFIDENCE.

"His Left Hand is under my head, and His Right Hand shall embrace me."—*Cant.* ii.

How calmly in Your Hands I rest
   When clouds are dark above me,
And never doubt You love me best
   When least You seem to love me!
For pain is still the "better part;"
   But how retain the feeling,
While You are whispering to the heart
   And all its worth revealing?

When sweetly mingled with Your own,
   There is no dart of sadness,
But thrills my spirit like a tone
   Of more celestial gladness:
But when that Heart is closed to me,
   And thus You leave me lonely,
'Tis then I feel my peace to be
   In pain and patience only.

Too oft Your Right Hand fails to bless
   With its divine embracing,
But on Your Left I lean no less,
   In this my safety placing:

Your tenderness may come and go,
   To try and tempt and prove me,
But, by Your strengthening grace, I know
   You have not ceased to love me.

ENGLAND.

England!—dear England!—to whom my heart cries,
With songs from my spirit and tears from my eyes;
Forgive if I e'er breathed a prayer for thy strand,
Save in yearning to see thee a Catholic land.

Alas! for that hunger, from pride taking birth,
For the homage of nations and riches of earth!
Ah! wide shall thy want and thy misery be,
While the Banquet of God is untasted by thee.

The wail of *our* orphans may plaintively rise,
There's a Mother that hears it far up in the skies,—
But where shall *thy* nurse and thy comfortress be,
If the kind hands of Mary be tied up by thee?

The grasp of the fever *our* homesteads may bare,
Our dead are not severed from kindness and care;
But alas! for *thy* lost ones, though dear they may be,
No still "De Profundis" is chanted by thee.

Thy wealth is unreal, poor desolate land!
While no flowers for Mary grow under thy hand,
And no light to thy poor in their sorrow can be,
While the Crucified Image no longer they see.

Fast fettered by sickness, I yet can implore
God's light on thy spirit to see and adore,
And the prayers of His saints for the true-hearted
    band
Who are striving to make thee a Catholic Land.

MOTHER OF CHRIST.

Oh, for a tongue to bless thy name!
   Oh, for a heart to love thee!
Whose crowning joy none else can claim,
   With nought but God above thee;
With eyes on Christ for ever set,
   And lips whose fearless pleading
Have never known denial yet,
   Though always interceding.

O mercy-seat! which God hath built
   For souls like mine to cry to:
O mother-heart! which shame or guilt
   Need never fear to fly to:
The Virgin always free from sin!
   That God might always hear thee;
The Mother of the thorn-crowned King!
   Lest sinful man should fear thee.

SAINT ROSE AND HER FLOWERS.

Saint Rose of Lima, who is herself called "The first *flower* of American sanctity," had a particular love for cultivating flowers for the altar.

Among her flowers the brightest flower,
   The youthful Rose goes by,
To pause beside the ruined bower,
   With many an anxious sigh;

Then, mingling tears and prayers, she fain
  Would vent her grief with God,
And wondering asks—"What foot profane
  My home of beauty trod?"

Mildly the lips of Jesus move—
  Sweetly the answer flows—
" I am the Flower that thou shouldst love,
  My own beloved Rose.
What—though My daily mercy showers
  Her countless gifts on thee—
My hand must strike thy brightest flowers
  When loved instead of *Me!*"

Oh! let us think when hopes are crossed
  And loftiest visions fall,
When life's best joys are dimmed or lost,
  How Jesus struck them all!
So shall we leave our ruined bowers,
  In gladness more than pain,
And joyful yield our fairest flowers
  That one sweet Flower may reign.

PHASES OF LOVE.

" Whoever loves knows the cry of this voice."—*Imit.* iii. 5.

O HOLY Love! O happy Love!
Which owns no joy itself above,
Which rests in labour, smiles in pain,
But finds its freedom in its chain;

Which cries to God with mighty power,
And wins for its eternal dower
A home in His all-bounteous Heart,
Secured by its resistless art.
      Jubilate.

True home of Love! true fount of bliss!
Teach me to spurn all love but this,
And fearless rise, and rest secure
Where love is just and joy is pure:
Filled with a fervour all divine,
Lift from myself this heart of mine,
Loose from its earthly bonds and ties,
To mingle with its native skies.
      Jubilate.

Teach me the songs that Angels sing;
Give me the love from which they spring;
With quenchless flame and always new,
Bid my poor heart leap up to You.
See how the waters glance and flow,
List how they murmur as they go;—
Thus would I seek my primal source,
Thus would I sing along my course,
      Jubilate.

Where shall I find this love so true?
Fearless and yet so fearful too,
Binding the thought lest thought should stray,
Guarding the sense, lest sense betray;
Patient to hear and slow to speak,
Faithful to suffer, quiet, meek,
Swift in obedience, and awake
To every form that God can take.
      Jubilate.

This love that burns within the breast
When tried as when by You caressed,
Glad in Your joy through its own pain,
And watching for Your voice again;
Leaning upon its lonely prayer,
Blessing Your will triumphant there,
Sure that the hopes which wait and wait
You will not long leave desolate.
      Jubilate.

Oh! for this Love of loves would I
Tormented live, or joyful die:
Choose then my life Your own right way,
Guide all my footsteps night and day;
Send every loss and every pain
Through which this love may freer reign.
What though my heart too loudly shriek!
Father! the human heart is weak;
But You can strengthen for the share
Of sorrow which You give to bear.
      Jubilate. Amen.

CHURCH FLOWERS.

Oh, the light that falls from Heaven's bright halls
 Upon holy Church below!
Oh, to Heaven above the song of love
 That from holy Church doth go!
Oh, the saints that pray in their cells to-day,
 And the joyful hymns that rise
On the incense-breath of a living faith,
 To their brethren in the skies!

Oh, the angels bright with their wings of light,
    And their whispering words of cheer,
That go·up and down from cross to crown,
    To make us a pathway clear!
Oh, the stories old of the martyrs bold,
    With their standard of faith unfurled,
Who went forth to die for the God on high,
    And the life of a better world!

Oh, the virgins pale, in the shadowy veil,
    All vowed to the Heavenly Lover,
For whom Christ doth stand with the crown in hand,
    Till their pilgrimage here is over!
Oh, the children fair that were snatched up there
    Ere sorrow or sin had broken!
And the matrons mild that gave up the child
    When the will of the Lord was spoken!

Oh, the glowing faith that through life and death
    Can the smile of a God discover!
Oh, the varying flowers of this Church of ours
    That blossom the two worlds over!
May we cherish them here with a love so dear
    That they'll bloom for us yet in Heaven,
Where the innocent stand in a glittering band,
    And the penitent smile forgiven.

THE ANSWERING PICTURE.

Hope was fast and faster sinking,
    Heaven had shut its face from me,
And my soul kept sadly thinking
    What her final doom might be:

Was she not abandoned by You
　　To life's dark and stormy main?
Then, when she had anchored nigh You,
　　Was she not cast forth again?
To mine eyes that moment stealing
　　Mournfully towards yonder wave,
You, who marked the secret feeling,
　　Swift the answering picture gave.

Out on the tide, with white sail flowing,
　　His tiny bark a young child threw—
Then, quickly to a distance rowing,
　　Let wind and wave their bidding do.
At first the light sail strove to aid her,
　　But quivering soon began to bow,
Nor ever dreamed the hand that made her
　　Was just as strong to save her now.
But when the wave, grown bold and bolder,
　　Had all but swept the trembler o'er,
Oh! he who formed was there to hold her
　　And take her to himself once more.

'Twas Your own kindly touch that found me!
　　I saw, rejoiced, and owned anew—
Life's storms may rise and rage around me,
　　' They ne'er can wreck in sight of *You*.

"THY WILL BE DONE."

YESTERDAY, the summer sunshine
　　Poured a full and noontide glow,
Forth I went, and all my glory
　　Was that Thou hadst willed it so:

Clouds to-day obscure that splendour,
   Why am I rejoicing still
But because this rain is only
   Servant of Thy mighty Will.

Oh! 'tis summer ever, always
   In our own eternal Home;
Could we rise to God's embraces
   Chill or change would never come:
Still that mighty Will adoring
   In morning breath or midnight roar;
Still that gracious Heart imploring
   But to love It more and more.

Would we pass from earth to Heaven,
   Would we taste the joys above,
Let us seek where Angels find them,—
   In the Will of Him they love.
Oh, what songs the Angels teach us!
   Oh, what triumph-tones they know!
Gladdening, with their glorious music,
   All this weary strife below.

Earth for them is not an exile,
   God is always smiling there,
All their life is filled with Heaven,
   Though earth's life they seem to share;
Gladly would they teach their secret,
   Gladly own what peace is won
From the thought—"'Tis God that wills it"—
   From the word—"His Will be done."

Oh! forbear our useless striving;
   God will reign, not I nor you,—
Let us then bow down adoring,
   Whate'er He does, or does not do:

Clasp we joy, 'tis He who gives it,
    Thank him with a joyful heart;
Sends He sorrow, oh! refuse not
    To embrace that better part.
Through both, with earnest, strong endeavour,
    Aim at, pray for only this,
That His Will may reign for ever,
    And our own be lost in His.

THE CURÉ D'ARS.

The Venerable John Baptist Vianney, whose life seemed a miracle of zealous labour and penance, died 1859.

I will not call thee "Blessed Saint,"
    Till holy Church shall say
That we may place thy image high,
    And at thine altar pray;
But I will call thee "chosen one,"
    And, through heart-faith in thee,
Invoke within my secret prayer
    Thy spirit down on me.

I think, indeed, if thou wert here
    Before mine eyes to-day,
The pride with which I've fought so long
    Would wholly melt away;
I'd do thy bidding at a sign,
    I'd stand, I'd come, I'd go—
The reason why the order came
    I'd never seek to know.

I would not feel my life at all
    If thou wert living here;
Before the Life that lived in thee
    My own would disappear;

I would not ask a word beyond
   What thou wast pleased to say,
But bless thy silence as thy speech,
   And do thy work all day.

There's nothing that can wound in thee;
   What should we strive with there?
The only arms that thou dost use
   Are vigils, tears, and prayer;
Thou weepest o'er the sinner's loss,
   Till he himself kneels down
And asks thee to remove at once
   His burden and thine own.

What hinders that the learned man
   In thee should seek a guide,
Who never can dispute with him
   The trophies of his pride?
Who to his claim will freely yield
   The praise of learning all,
While holding to his steps a light
   Whose rays beyond it fall!

Who fears, howe'er devoid of good,
   His secret soul to show
To one who in his own eyes lies
   A thousand times more low?
Who grudges power to him whose grace
   Is all for others' aid,
Whose brow seems always sinking 'neath
   The crowns upon it laid?

O Curé d'Ars! for three whole years
   I've pined thy life to know,
And now the book is in my hands,
   I cannot farther go;

By slow degrees I'll read it all,
    As one who on the way
Must pause, and pause at every step,
    To wonder and to pray.

But bless me as I still read on,—
    For every good I seek,
A steady toil, a patient prayer,
    An humble heart and meek,
A loving heart, whose love will yet
    In God's own order glow,
Until I find within myself
    His kingdom here below.

A living faith will rule my life,
    While hope and faith will aid
A joyous welcome of the cross,
    And peace when on it laid;
With grace to every passing grace
    So faithful still to be,
That I shall grow the *very saint*
    God wants to find in me.

CROSS AND CROWN.

Look up to your God with a worshipful heart
    Which eagerly thirsts for His call;
Ask not in measure, and give not in part,
    But offer Him all for all;
Shun not the cross as too great to bear,
    God knows what His grace can do;
Doubt not the crown as too bright to wear,
    Its glory was meant for you.

Dare, since the sainted are saints by love,
   To tread in the King's highway,
And ask from the mercy of God above
   To love like a saint to-day:
Ask with a courage, alive and true,
   And let not your hope grow dim—
For what though the least be too much for you,
   Is the greatest enough for Him?

Oh! teach me to act on the words I say,
   To live by the truths I know,
And royally walk in the royalest way
   By which all the sainted go.
Shape thou the cross, be it heavy or light,
   But with it give strength to bear;
Weave Thou the crown, be it ever so bright,
   Thou'lt lift up the brow to wear.

VIATICUM.

Though to clasp Thee, Lord, so often
   Every sorrow seems to soften,
Yet, I long that day to see
   When, for my last journey starting,
   I will shed few tears at parting—
Save in joy to go with Thee.

O my dear Conductor! guide me
   Where Thou wilt when once beside me;
Through death's darkness sweet to be
   Cast upon Thy dear protection,
   Clasped by all Thy kind affection
Closer, and more bound to Thee!

Oh! what foe can overmatch me?
Who from Thy right hand shall snatch me?
What can bind whom Thou dost free?
  Yes! though it be wintry weather,
  Let us journey forth together,
Thou for Heaven, and I for Thee.

MOURN FOR THE HOLY IMAGES.

Mourn for the holy Images
  That held their quiet rule
Of peace and love and purity,
  Above our convent school!
We taught the little hands to work,
  We taught the lips to pray,
The sweet face of the Virgin—best
  Knew how the hearts to sway.

Oh! when these youthful minds are stirred
  By passions, dark and wild,
Where can we point to Jesus now,
  The meek and silent Child?
'Tis true we tell them how He sat
  And smiled on Mary's knee,
But children are so slow to learn
  The things they do not see!

And, when the sweet month comes again,
  In which they used to pray
And sing their hymns round Mary's shrine,
  The loving Queen of May,
We'll blush before their eager eyes,
  If they should ask us where
They'll bring their lights and garlands now,
  And sing their darling prayer.

And we, O God! Thou knowest how oft,
  In strife of heart and brain,
We've turned us to that Image dear,
  That love might conquer pain;
Then for the sake of Him who sat
  Upon the Virgin's knee,
Turned smiling to our work again,
  Because we worked for Thee.

Now, ours is like an earthly school
  Where this cold world hath trod,
And struck with hand of iron down
  The holy things of God:
The lettered tablet courts our view,
  The map is on the wall;
But, oh! to look where Mary's face
  Once brightened over all!

Take back your cold and cautious books,
  Unwarmed by loving prayers;
Take back your systems wisely planned
  To spare our pious cares;
Take back your gold and give to us
  Our poverty, our pain—
The Image of the Virgin sweet
  With her loved Child again!

FETTERS.

I AM Your creature, and aspire
  Your holy will to do,
I am Your subject, and desire
  No other Lord but you.

I am the friend for whom You gave
    Your Life-Blood, full and free;
I am Your purchase and Your slave—
    Oh, never part with me.

I am Your daughter, still 'tis You
    My every need supply;
I am Your sister, since You drew
    To my weak nature nigh.

I am Your captive, whom Your grace
    Must more and more control,
Still conquering till it leaves no trace
    Of *me* within my soul.

I am Your spouse, but this last tie
    Not yet makes sure of Heaven,
And I must tremble till I die,
    With fetters all unriven.

SAINT TERESA WATCHING THE BLESSED SACRAMENT.

To guard her God Teresa rose,
    At work for Him all day;
By night she broke her short repose
    To watch Him where He lay.
She could not sleep with fearing still
    That sacrilegious sword
Was busy at its work of ill,
    To rob her of her Lord.

The moon had just begun to shine
 And lit the scene like day,
Till she could see the ruined shrine
 In which her Saviour lay;
For what, though many a guard was set
 To sentinel the wall,
With fearing they might slumber yet,
 She could not rest at all.

Since Mary while the Infant slept
 Looked down in trembling bliss,
What heart for God hath ever kept
 A truer watch than this?
Oh! triumph of the creature's love,
 When thrilled with tenderest fear,
She sees the Eternal God above
 In her sole keeping here!

But is it not for hearts whose fire
 Hath caught this quenchless glow,
The Hidden God can still desire
 To fix His home below?
For every age, by sword or tongue,
 Would desolate His shrine,
And every land its dart hath flung
 In hate of things divine;

But *some* will always rise by night
 To keep their vigil true,
Till Angels gaze, with hushed delight,
 On human watchers too;
And fast as foes are darkening round,
 Some hearts will always dare
To guard the altar's sacred ground,
 Like Saint Teresa's prayer.

SOLITUDE.

Sweet and strange it is to be
So helplessly alone with Thee,
Without a friend, without an aid,
Tempted, trembling, and afraid,
Holding by Thy hand, and so
Looking in Thine eyes, as though
To Thy Heart my own would say,
" Pity this poor castaway."

Yes, 'tis in these hours of fear
That I feel Thee, God! most near,
Feel Thine every breath and tone,
While I wait on them alone,
Feel how well it is for me
Here to dwell alone with Thee
Whom alone I yet must meet,
At the awful judgment-seat.

SERVANTS OF MARY.

While Bernard and Alphonsus cry,
  With trumpet-voice, aloud
The glories of the Queen of Saints,
  And preach her to the crowd—
Saint Louis and Saint Stanislaus,
  By her low breathings fanned,
As timidly as young spring flowers,
  Grow up beneath her hand.

While Bernard and Alphonsus raise
  Her banner in the light,
Like Mary's champions, battling for
  Her glory and her right—

Saint Louis and Saint Stanislaus
  In hidden life and sweet,
Like Mary's children tenderly
  Her daily praise repeat.

Where unbelieving words are rife
  And Christian hearts are cold,
For Mary's honour may we be,
  Like Saint Alphonsus, bold;
When ignorance and doubt assail
  From ill-instructed men,
Oh! may we share in Mary's cause
  Saint Bernard's unction then:

But when the galling irksomeness
  Of humble works we feel,
And pride assumes the ready guise
  Of courage or of zeal,
Oh! let us then be mindful how,
  In daily life unseen,
Saint Louis and Saint Stanislaus
  Gave glory to their Queen.

LINES WRITTEN IN BLESSED HENRY SUSO'S* "LITTLE BOOK OF THE ETERNAL WISDOM."

In tracking through thy spirit-world
  A strange delight I took,
Yet know not if I understood,
  Or only felt thy Book:

* A celebrated mystical writer of the Order of Saint Dominic.

For ever is thy wisdom set
　　To such melodious air,
The music winds into my soul
　　And weaves the moral there.

I listen to the " Golden Harp "
　　Which sounds so far above,
And, by its varying cadences
　　I regulate my love;
For when I miss the charmed words,
　　No less the air can show
If I should laugh exultingly,
　　Or wring my hands for woe.

The incense-breath of opening flowers,
　　The music born of birds,
And all the warmth of summer joys
　　Are in thy woven words:
It seems some angel-talisman
　　Is lent thee from above,
Who still, through earthly images,
　　Infusest heavenly love.

Or, do familiar joys indeed,
　　With unknown sweetness, grow
Round heights which seem so bare to eyes
　　That scan them from below?
Do jocund beam and wreathing flower
　　Of tenfold charm delight
The spirit-gaze, which opens on
　　Perfection's awful height?

Whatever secret dwells therein
　　One fact can all descry,—
Thou hast not left thy joys behind,
　　In mounting thus so high;

But rather do the mellowing chords
   Of thy rich harp declare
That all we dream of love and joy
   Is "real life" when there.

THE SECRET OF THE SAINTS.

To play through life a perfect part,
   Unnoticed and unknown;
To seek no rest in any heart
   Save only God's alone;
In little things to own no will,
   To have no share in great,
To find the labour ready still,
   And for the crown to wait.

Upon the brow to bear no trace
   Of more than common care,
To write no secret in the face
   For men to read it there;
The daily cross to clasp and bless,
   With such familiar zeal
As hides from all that not the less
   The daily weight you feel.

In toils that praise will never pay
   To see your life go past,
To meet in every coming day
   Twin sister of the last;
To hear of high, heroic things,
   And yield them reverence due,
But feel life's daily offerings
   Are far more fit for you.

To woo no secret, soft disguise
    To which self-love is prone,
Unnoticed by all other eyes,
    Unworthy in your own;
To yield with such a happy art
    That no one thinks you care,
And say to your poor, bleeding heart—
    "How little you can bear!"

Oh! 'tis a pathway hard to choose,
    A struggle hard to share,
For human pride would still refuse
    The nameless trials there;
But since we know the gate is low
    That leads to heavenly bliss,
What higher grace could God bestow
    Than such a life as this?

TO THE REBUKING ANGELS.

"Why stand you looking up to Heaven?"—Acts i. 11

For this we stand, for this we gaze,—
    Because our Lord passed by,
And left a track of light which still
    Doth linger in the sky:
For this we stand, for this we gaze,
    Until that light shall glow
Within our souls, to cheer us through
    The way we've yet to go.

Oh! do not chide our faltering steps,
    Though in no haste to part
From the warm breath of life, which still
    Doth play about our heart;

We shall not be the less prepared
  For battle-front and fray,
Because, with many a fond regret,
  We linger here to day.

SUNSHINE THROUGH SHOWERS.

O Lord! how it cheers to remember through all,
  Though grief be the pathway, that bliss is the goal,—
Though shadows may scare us and spectres appal,
  That sunshine with rest is the home of the soul;
Though brief are our pleasures, they sweetly remind
  Of the transports eternal prepared by thy love,
And, when pain is the darkest, what peace we can find
  In the thought that it leads to such glory above!

Yes, life at the saddest has sweetness in store
  For those who will take it as coming from Thee,
Will smile on their joys, and when they pass o'er,
  Turn, smiling as ever, their sorrow to see;
Will say—" Since life's changes should never destroy
  The sweet, even spirit Thy children must know,
And since 'tis so hard to look solemn in joy,—
  Oh! grant us the grace to look cheerful in woe."

FATHER LOUIS DA PONTE.

Saint Dominic trained and nurtured him
  With early lessons deep,
Then passed to Saint Ignatius,
  Through his after-life to keep;

As if a precious jewel first
    To Mary's hand were given,
And she should yield it tenderly
    To her sweet Son in Heaven.

Yet much it cost his heart to lay
    His early dream aside,
And drink from other streams than those
    Which first his youth supplied;
The masters who instructed him,
    The saints to whom he prayed,
The Rule which he so long had loved,
    And fain would have obeyed.

He knew not what was thwarting him,
    And urging him to see
The Order which Ignatius built
    Should *his* election be:
The new was ever bare to him,
    And fain he would have sought
A home where mild antiquity
    Her starry spell-work wrought;

But grace achieved her triumph, and,
    With spirit all resigned,
He went to fight his battle
    Where his Captain had assigned;
Nor was interior struggle long
    Before him ere he found—
That God supplies the arms when He
    Is left to choose the ground.

From love to holy Dominic
    He was never seen to part,
And the zeal for Mary's honour
    Was a passion in his heart;

But his soul at death appearing
  In the light of glory drest—
Shone the blessed Name of Jesus,
  Like a jewel on his breast.

COMFORT.

Thou rememb'rest that eve when the sunset was throwing
  Its light on the picture that hung o'er Thy shrine?
Thy face was all dark, but Thy Heart was all glowing,
  And the gloom and the radiance alike were divine:
I had knelt at Thy feet in too heavy a sadness,
  My soul quivered under the weight of its woe,
But one glance at that picture upraised it in gladness,
  And I saw 'twas thy love had inflicted the blow.

O Lord! since Thy Face is in shadow so often,
  The glow of Thy Heart let me sometimes behold,
That the thought of Its love every sorrow may soften
  Till the days of this wearisome exile be told;
And still, as each year its own anguish is bringing,
  And hope after hope I am forced to resign,
Bid me think of that eve when the sunset was flinging
  Such light on the picture that hung o'er Thy shrine.

SAINT ELIZABETH OF HUNGARY.

Upon her young and childlike brow
   A morning sunshine stole,
Which sent the mist from every heart,
   The cloud from every soul;
When lifting up her royal eyes,
   She stood in noble mien—
As mild as any maiden, but
   As grand as any queen.

A princess by the right of birth;
   In marriage she was crowned
As duchess of Thuringia wide,
   And ruled o'er all its ground;
For good Duke Louis still would leave
   His treasures in her care,
When boundless alms gave ample proof,
   Of who was mistress there.

And everywhere about the land
   The holy buildings rose,
To which the sick and poor might come
   For healing and repose;
While royal hands make smooth the bed
   And tend the foul disease—
For who is like Elizabeth
   At kindly works like these?

How often, from the banquet missed,
   Within her room she sate,
Because her mantle had been craved
   By beggar at the gate!

Or passed to high, Church-festival
   The glove from off her hand,
Because her purse had emptied been
   Before the last demand!

Yet many a playful miracle
   Did love divine show forth,
That while she only lived for Heaven,
   She might not fail on earth;
And sometimes Angels yield her back
   The alms which they receive,
And sometimes clothe her in the robes
   Which only they can weave.

Her household life, serene and pure,
   I will not pause to tell,
Yet is there one sweet scene whereon
   My fancy loves to dwell,
In which the gentle husband vowed.
   To strive, as best he could,
To aid his weeping saint to reach
   Still greater heights of good.

And soon, how soon! his word he kept—
   By yielding up the life
Which made the one strong tie to earth
   For that devoted wife:
When, fast the shoots began to spring
   Of every highest grace,
And love divine could triumph in
   Its consecrated place.

Chased rudely from her palace walls
   By calumny and wrong,
Her children clinging round her steps,
   Elizabeth passed on;

And, when the poor her hands had fed
   Heaped insults on her way,
Her noble heart rejoiced to be
   A poorer still than they.

If nature felt a mighty pang
   To hear the children's plaint,
The *mother's* sorrow only fed
   The patience of the *saint;*
And, when her children shared no more
   The path by which she trod
And smiled for other eyes than hers,
   She seemed to fly to God.

The world again its honours brought
   To brow so mildly sweet,
And royal heart and diadem
   Were offered at her feet;
But light she held imperial rank,
   By nobler bridals won,
And fast she kept her plighted faith
   To God's Eternal Son.

Yet, when in bloom of youth she died,
   And wonder, work, and sign
Cast light upon her sanctity—
   Drew homage to her shrine,
Once more that knightly emperor
   With loyal speed, went forth,
And crowned *her* with the crown of Heaven,
   Who shunned the crown of earth.

If in Elizabeth you seek
   The ruling grace to find—
With mercy to the poor of Christ
   Her very heart seemed twined;

But fearing still herself in all,
  She cast both heart and soul,
In vowed obedience, down beneath
  The rod of strong control.

And thus, methinks, should every heart
  Whose chosen gift would sway,
With bit and bridle see it bound
  While learning to obey;
For nature, e'en in holy things,
  Disputes the reign with God;
And blind obedience is the path
  That He Himself has trod.

THE MEETING.

They tell me thought can never shape the strange, mysterious woe
Thy justice hath prepared for souls unpurified below;
That years of keenest torture here were light indeed to bear,
When set beside the mildest stroke which is inflicted there.

Yet, Lord! I do not reason thus, in asking still of Thee
Such purifying suffering here as Thou shalt choose for me:
And, should it but increase my pains, I here would rather wait,
Than go to meet Thee with my soul in such a piteous state.

Oh, woe! to see my Spouse come forth, and hide my
    drooping face—
Ashamed to let Him see the soul which He could not
    embrace,—
To feel that in the bridal hour I must to exile go,
And pass from all His tenderness to prison-chains
    below.

My Lord! my Love! what wonder, if I smile the
    rod to see
Whose every stroke prepares me for Thy first ap-
    proach to me?
What wonder, if that rapturous hour can light up
    every woe,
Until I scarcely feel the pangs which fit my soul to go!

THE ANGELIC DOCTOR.

Saint Thomas was a ruler grand
    Who swayed by word and pen,
And boldly held his light in hand
    To cheer the hearts of men :
He learned no lesson from the crowd
    But soared beyond their reach,
And fearless spoke the Truth aloud
    When going forth to teach.

Saint Thomas had his learning-tools,
    His books and papers too,
And yet 'twas not from human schools
    His wondrous lights he drew,—
But there, where schools and masters fail,
    Cast humbly on the sod,
He bade the power of prayer prevail,
    To wrest the truth from God.

Saint Thomas, in his loftiest flight,
    No vain presumption knew,
So, God was free to pour the light
    His taintless spirit through;
For, while a dreaming world awoke
    Beneath his kindling thought,
He but admired the truths he spoke,
    And held himself for nought.

Saint Thomas kept his aim in sight
    At every dart he sped,
Nor ever missed his purpose right,
    Whatever road it led:
Swift answering, when his gracious Lord
    Looked down benignantly
And bade him name his own reward—
    "None other, Lord, but Thee."

Saint Thomas is the Patron grand
    For all who write and teach;
They, too, should learn throughout the land
    To keep the word they preach;
So shall the crown shine brightly yet
    For which their labours call,
And God Eternal pay the debt
    He fain would owe to all.

FESTIVAL GROUND.

The Temples! the Temples! to name them at all,
What quick-thronging visions respond to the call!
What prayer and what blessings gush forth at the sound,
For our souls are in love with their Festival Ground!

We remember the time when as children we prayed,
All awed by their glory and pleased with their shade,
When we felt the first thrill of devotion and fear—
The fast-growing sense of a Deity near;
The lights on the altar, the Saints on the wall,
The wonderful music which burst over all,
The voice of the preacher unfolding the Law,
Till we melted with sorrow or trembled with awe.
We pass on to the day when the altar was drest,
And the children went forth to the Festival blest,
When our hearts clasped their Saviour in closest embrace,
Till, like Peter on Thabor, we clung to the place.

We remember the time, when in sadness and shame,
Again to the shade of these Temples we came—
Our promises broken, our fealty forswore,
And no light but the hope of their welcome once more.
Were they deaf to our pleadings or blind to our tears?
Did they leave us unaided, to anguish and fears?
Did they coldly remind us that traitors must meet
The doom they have earned by their wilful deceit?
O Lord of the Temples! Thy love was the same
When the children knelt down and the penitent came—
But its warmth and assurance still tenderer grew,
As our guilt and our treason looked blacker in hue.

O Lord of the Temples! what wonder if we
Should weep, with warm love, their least vestige to see,
Should bring all our treasures of fondness and prayer,
Of lights and of flowers for offerings there;

Should hail them with rapture, should name them
    with pride,
In the war of the scoffer should stand by their side;
Should cry, though the world stood sneering around,
That our souls are in love with their Festival
    Ground!

MAGDALEN'S LOVE.

O THOU who wouldst not quit the trace
    Of where thy Lord hath been,
Still hanging o'er the vacant place,—
    His grief-struck Magdalen!

When first his saving accents sweet
    Thy tearful trance dispelled,
And, fond, thou turnedst to clasp His feet,—
    'Twas hard to be repelled!

But love, elated overmuch,
    Could joy itself control;
The word that stayed thy eager touch
    Enkindled all thy soul.

So swift the tender grace to seek,
    So calm the check to bear,
So meekly warm, so boldly meek,—
    Fit type of love and prayer!

Fain would my soul the ardours prove
    Which drew thee to His side,—
Still more she needs the patient love
    That bore to be denied!

TO SAINT RAPHAEL.

Spirit of the spirits seven,
Sweetly linking earth to Heaven,
'Tis the holy name you bear
Makes us hope for all your care.

I am always sick and weak,
But the gift of health I seek
Is that pain itself may be
Source of purest life to me.

While I dwell in shadows here,
Set my inner vision clear;
And, though bound in every limb,
Bid my spirit soar to Him.

"Cure of God,"—bright spirit, who
Are the guide of pilgrims too,
Far too blind to see my way,
Guidance at your hands I pray.

On the road of sorrow cast
Let me hold my footing fast,
Nor from noonday toil or heat
Ever turn to rest my feet.

By the road of sorrow led,
Meek and thankful may I tread,
Thinking, every step I go,
How my Saviour walked below.

Spirit of the spirits seven,
Cure of God and guide to Heaven,
All the health for which I care
Is enough to take me there.

DARKNESS.

O Lord, I do not ask Thee now
    To quiet nor console,
I cannot suffer, save when Thou
    Art silent in my soul;
I'm tired of grief this many a day,
    My pains I cannot speak,
But on Thy Heart my own to lay
    Is all the rest I seek.

If I could see Thy Heaven of love
    Far in the future shine,
How high 'twould lift my soul above
    Those phantom pains of mine!
But darkness all beyond me spread,
    And darkness all around,
Where can I lay my aching head
    Save where Thy own was bound.

I ask Thee not, through life's short hour,
    One solace to impart,
But bless each pain, and give it power
    To purify my heart;
Dark though my life, 'twere darker far,
    At close of life, to see
Death come to break my prison-bar,
    But not to set me free.

BLESSED JAMES OF MEVANIA.
OF THE ORDER OF ST. DOMINIC.

Being illustrious for preaching and miracles, and receiving on all sides praise and honour, Blessed James was penetrated by fear of the judgments of God, and apprehensive of losing his soul. (Died 1301.)

Souls that never tasted bliss
    Little dread to lose it,
All their question comes to this—
    "Shall I *quite* refuse it?"

Souls that love—how sadly fear
  Not to love for ever,
When they cling most fondly near,
  Fearing most to sever.

Shades of night were gathering fast,—
  Lonely vigil keeping,
Close beside the Altar cast,
  A saint, in fear, was weeping:
Nights of prayer no solace brought,
  Days of high endeavour,—
Still he asked, with ceaseless thought,
  "Shall I love for ever?"

In this hour of wordless woe,
  All night's shadows near him,
Christ in pity looked below,
  Taking thought to cheer him;
From the Crucifix out-gushed
  On his prostrate form,
Stream of Blood—which, falling, hushed
  All his spirit's storm.

Words he heard, of joyful flow,
  Through his bosom welling—
"Take this covenant, and know
  Heaven shall be thy dwelling."
O dear Lord! what peace came down
  On his heart of terror,
Waked so sweetly by Thine own
  From its dream of error;

Stilling many an anxious thought
  With their breathings holy;—
Such high wonders are not wrought
  For the sainted solely!

Ne'er gushed out with freer flow
    Christ's dear Blood o'er any,
Than when Calvary's hill of woe
    Poured it out for " many."

Every time the Mass-bell rings,
    His true word is given,
And the gush of Life-Blood brings
    Sign of peace from Heaven.
Ever thus, my soul can find
    Under all the glory,
Something for herself designed
    In each saintly story.

MY THREE ACTS.

O Lord! I know the pains I prove
Are but the tokens of Thy love;
The tears, so frequent and so free,
But signs that Thou rememb'rest me.

I know that if I come at last
To Heaven, where sighs and tears are past,
My grateful heart will thank and praise
For all life's dark and thorny ways:

But, wherefore till that hour delay
The tribute of my thanks to pay?
While Faith points out the road to me,
When I receive the cross from Thee.

So, first I bow beneath the rod
Of thy chastising hand, my God!
And own the sinner at thy feet
A heavier stroke deserves to meet.

And next, with all my heart, I bless
Thy kind and thoughtful tenderness,
As all in love the cross I see,
Which comes to make me like to Thee.

And then, with exultation high,
I snatch the coin with which to buy
Eternal bliss and queenly state,
And buy them at so cheap a rate.

Oh, no! I will not wait to see
In Heaven what pain has done for me;
In midnight darkness faith can show
That all is good Thou dost bestow.

QUEEN OF MARTYRS.

Why didst Thou walk the earth so long
  After the Crucified?
How wast thou pleased to linger on,
  When thy heart's-life had died?
Still to thine eye that death-scene rose,
  Still to thine ear that cry:—
How, Mother, didst thou bear such woes,
  Nor bow thy head and die?

God willed it, therefore thou didst will;—
  For this thy Son was given;
For this thou art a mourner still,
  When He is crowned in Heaven.
For this content to linger on,
  Resigned to God's decree;
Thou canst not think that exile long
  Which He assigns to thee.

Lord! who didst mark those weary years,
  And weigh that heavy chain,
Accept for me her secret tears,
  And all her silent pain;
That I may sweetly drink the cup
  Thy hand has filled for me,
And still, like Mary, offer up
  Life's martyrdom for Thee.

STRENGTH BEFORE SWEETNESS.

Sweet is the grace of possession,
But strong is the grace of privation;—
Order my life as Thou wilt,
God, who upholdest creation;
Close to Thy Heart and Thy love,
Calmed by Thy quiet caresses,—
Fighting Thy battles afar
When fiercest temptation oppresses.

Sweet is the grace of possession,
But strong is the grace of privation:—
Just as thy God shall ordain
Ever, my soul, be thy station:
Rest on His Heart in thy love,
Hold by His hand in thy terror;
He can delight thee with truth,
He can defend thee from error.

Sweet is the grace of possession,
But strong is the grace of privation;—
Give thyself up to thy God,
And trust in thy proper vocation.

Courtiers stay close to their king,
Soldiers go forth to befriend him,—
Those shall have served at his feet,
These shall have bled to defend him.

Sweet is the grace of possession,
But strong is the grace of privation ;—
Light out of darkness shall dawn,
And chaos give place to creation :
Love is the lesson for all,
Humbleness, faith, and endeavour,—
Then give to us pleasure or pain,
God is our portion for ever !

WEEDS AND FLOWERS.

THERE are weeds and there are flowers
   Springing from the same green sod,
Flying birds and creeping insects
   Are alike Thy work, O God !
There seems neither use nor beauty
   In a thousand things we see,
Yet, we know they have a purpose,
   Since they all were sent by Thee.

With this thought my soul I quiet,
   When she fain would ask me why
I am left so long a burden
   To the earth and to the sky;
Neither vowed to pain nor labour,
   Neither fit to think nor pray,
But a helpless body resting,
   With a useless mind all day.

With the weeds and with the insects
  I will take my place below,
Never asking any reason
  But that God has willed it so;
Should they trample or reject me,
  I will never dare complain,—
Knowing well that birds and flowers
  Have alone the right to reign.

THE ROYAL NAME OF MARY.

Sing for the men whose fearless pen
  Was never known to vary,
Nor pause to weigh how much 'twould say
  In love and praise to Mary.

They gave her Name a world-wide fame,
  They raised to Heaven her story,
But ne'er could reach what God would teach,
  If He should tell her glory.

Who dares to say that God must weigh
  The gifts of grace He'll render,
Lest He should light a thing so bright
  As to outshine His splendour?

Who dares to think, that He would shrink
  Nor crown, o'er every other,
The one whose claim lay in the Name
  And Royal right of Mother?

Then bless the men whose fearless pen
  Was never known to vary,
But still to write, in dazzling light,
  The Royal Name of Mary.

They gave her Name a world-wide fame,
    They sketched from Heaven her story,
But ne'er could reach what God will teach,
    When He shall tell her glory.

ETERNITY TRANSMUTES.

They have passed, or are passing, away and away,
In the chill of the twilight they care not to stay,
And afraid of the night, with its storms and its woes,
How they droop down their eyelids and sink to repose!

Some, too, were called hence in the fulness of noon,
No tears did they shed but for parting so soon
With the bird-notes so clear and the rose-hues so bright,—
Oh! they fain would have lingered in music and light.

How long I am watching! How many have died
That I saw in their vigour and strength by my side!
Oh! they felt for my weakness and grieved for my doom,
But 'tis I am the mourner, and they in the tomb.

What land hath received them? What shore do they tread?
Oh! various the countries that wait for the dead.
What thoughts are they thinking? What deeds would they show,
If again they returned to this exile below?

Oh! how, like bright gems, would they gather and prize
The tears that run down from our sorrowful eyes!
How the sickness that frets and the troubles that try
Would be dearer to them than the sun to the sky.

Oh! pleasure might fawn, like a slave, on the ground,
But 'tis pain that for them would be sceptred and crowned,
Till, when most they had wept in her service all day,
They would ask, in the night-time, new tears for their pay.

O Lord! to my weakness such thoughts will arise,
Yet, they change not my sorrow, they check not my sighs—
But though faith cannot lighten the burden I bear,
She can school me to patience, or lift me in prayer.

THE WELCOME VISITOR.

O Death! thou art gentle and faithful,
   O Death! thou art welcome and dear,
O Death! thou art pleasant and grateful
   To those who are suffering here.
Thy scythe is still swift to destroy
   Whatever it lights on below—
It cuts from the rich man his joy,
   It sweeps from the poor man his woe.

Oh! still be my heart of the number,
   That look for thy coming in peace,
Not long can the sorrow encumber
   Which, at thy first bidding, must cease

Thy scythe is most welcome to sever
  My soul from its banishment here,—
The stroke but unites me for ever
  With all that my spirit holds dear.

O Death! thou art gentle and faithful,
  O Death! thou are welcome and dear,
O Death! thou art pleasant and grateful
  To those who are suffering here.
If first, as a curse, thou wast given,
  With Christ a new era began,
And changed to the "portal of Heaven!"
  What friend should be dearer to man?

Oh! what could console me for staying
  If God had not ordered it so?
For this I endure the delaying
  While counting the moments below.
Thy scythe is still shining before me,
  Impatient to free me from earth,
Thy voice is still echoing o'er me,—
  Oh! when shall it summon me forth?

O Death! thou art gentle and faithful,
  O Death! thou art welcome and dear,
O Death! thou art pleasant and grateful
  To those who are suffering here.
For thee let the chamber be lighted,
  For thee let the banquet be set—
For, never hath sorrow invited
  A kinglier comforter yet!

THE PRAYER OF FATHER DOMINIC.

Saith Saint Dominic to his chosen,
  "If the seed be put to keep,
It will moulder to corruption,
  And no fruit shall any reap."

Saith Saint Dominic to his chosen,
  "If the seed be cast abroad,
It will bring forth in due season
  For the reaping hand of God."

Then, in wonder at his boldness,
  But all trusting to his word,
His little flock divided
  For the mission of the Lord;

And it calmed the grief of parting
  From their Master and their home,
To think upon their Saviour,
  And the harvest-time to come.

But one bent down all trembling
  And, beseeching not to go,
Said, his thought was ever feeble,
  And his speech was ever slow;

He looked to no conversion
  And he dreamed of no reward,
He feared but to dishonour
  The high mission of the Lord:

Then Saint Dominic, kindly soothing,
  Laid a blessing on his head,
And, "twice before the Altar
  I will think of thee," he said;

"At the sunrise and the sunset,
  Still a father's prayer shall be
That the God for whom thou strivest
  May be armour unto thee."

Then the young man rose up strengthened
  And went forth upon his way,
And, *he* never failed in preaching
  Who dared simply to obey;

But the fervour of his feeling
  And the grandeur of his word
Still gave proof that Father Dominic
  Was in prayer before the Lord.

THE WAYS OF GOD.

When God inspired Teresa's heart
  To shun the haunts of men,
She heard His voice, and talked apart
  With holy angels then:—
You sick and homeless hearts, that pine
  In search of human love,
It is no less a voice divine
  Which calls you from above.

When friends fall off and hearts grow cold,
  And earthly pleasures dim,
'Tis God who kindly breaks their hold,
  To fix your hope on Him;
And, oh! if like Teresa, too,
  You did His word obey,
Then Angels soon would glad your view,
  And brighten round your way.

A thousand ways the voice divine
    Doth thrill the listening soul,
A thousand lights from Heaven downshine
    To lead us to our goal;
On some God beams in vision clear,
    To some He speaks aloud;
At times, He whispers in the ear
    To draw them from the crowd:

And yet there is no surer call
    Than pain and sorrow speak,
No more convincing proof to all—
    That God the soul doth seek.
Then, let your fading stars depart,
    And, when they've left the skies,
In light and warmth upon your heart
    The blessed Sun will rise.

HOME-SICKNESS.

From the storms, from the darkness, oh, call me, my Love!
To Thy bright Home of beauty which smiles from above;
Or teach my poor spirit to brook the delay,
And patiently suffer till summoned away.

How fair, in Thy Heaven, the daylight must shine
Upon hearts that once sorrowed as darkly as mine!
How sweetly the songs of the Angels must fall,
When the voice of the tempest no more can appal!

Through the far-echoed music my heart seems to know
A rest from her labours a lull to her woe;

Yet sighs through her dreamings till summoned by Thee,
Where those joyful Hosannahs her welcome shall be.

ASSUMPTION MORNING.

Oh! sing, for our Queen is enthroned in the sky,
And the banners of mercy are waving on high;
And the ranks of the Blessed shine bright in the ray
Of the glory that breaks upon Heaven to-day.

Oh! sing for the captives from prison released,
Their bondage is over, their wailing hath ceased;
At the prayers of the Mother, the children are free,
And they rise, her companions in glory to be:

Oh! sing for earth's sinners, more fatally bound,
Their star is arisen when Mary is crowned;
Though the bright 'Sun of Justice' should awe by Its light,
The moonlight of Mary may guide them aright.

Yes, sing, though our hearts were as dark as the tomb,
The light of this morning should break on their gloom;
For, sad as the weight of our fetters may be,
How it thrills to remember that Mary is free!

How it thrills to remember, though wounded and bound
The children may languish, the Mother is crowned!
Oh! the heart of a Mother, the hand of a Queen
Won't long leave the children in bondage, I ween.

But sing for that Mother, her tears are no more,
Her sorrows have ended, her partings are o'er;
Nor all the bright Angels a glory have won
Like the crown which the Mother receives from the Son.

Sing, sing for the lips that for ever will be
Unwearied in pleading the captive to free,
And sing for the eyes that can never behold
A dearth at the table, but Jesus is told;

And sing for the heart that is quickest to feel,
And sing for the hands that are surest to heal,
And sing for the feet that will never be slow,
On the errand of mercy delighted to go.

Oh! yes, though our hearts were as dark as the tomb,
The bright light of this morning should break through their gloom;
For though we lay groaning like slaves on the ground,
We should leap in our fetters, for Mary is crowned.

A SONG OF THE SEASONS.

Like the singing of birds in the forest,
    As gladsome, spontaneous, and free,
My spirit delights to flow over,
    And sing out its love-notes to Thee.
The sun and the breeze and the branches
    Invite the wood-songsters to sing,
And I too am glad of the summer
    Because 'tis the breath of my King.

Oh! wide is creation around me;
   And everything fair that I see
Invites me to love Thee for ever,
   Since all were created for me.
The skies, in their noontide of splendour,
   All shining with azure and gold,
Present but a glimpse of Thy glory,
   In magical mirror unrolled.

O God! Thou art artist for ever,
   Still painting Thy pictures so bright,—
The Fountain of music and sunshine,—
   The centre of love and delight:
Yet, dearer by far than the summer,
   The woods or the wood-notes to me,
The snows and the ice of the winter,
   When bearing its rigours for Thee.

HOURS OF IDLENESS.

How she sits in her sable weeds, mourning
   With anguish no words can express,
Her heart and her eyes ever turning
   To the Kingdom she yet shall possess;
Her lips are too feeble for praying,
   Her voice cannot reach to the skies;
And there, in her grief, she is staying
   Till *you* shall have bid her arise.

Oh, friends! when your moments are wear
   You ask me what good they can do?
Look down to that Prison so dreary
   Whose gates can be opened by you:

Your prayers are a key never-failing;
  Then shut not your ears to the cry,
But send some poor soul from her wailing,
  To plead for your spirit on high.

WISHES.

Oh, that my heart a temple were where I could always stay!
Oh, that my thoughts, like Angels pure, would never cease to pray!
Oh, that my life, like some lone stream, still hurrying to the sea,
From hour to hour, with all its power, would ever tend to Thee!—

  My prayer is answered but in part;
  Each morn Thy shrine is in my heart;
  Yet not the less throughout the day,
  Some wandering thoughts forget to pray;
  And, though my life would gladly be
  The tide for ever set to Thee,
  O Lord! 'tis only Thou canst say
  How oft it wanders from the way.

THE BELL.

There is a Bell within my room,
  And silent though it be
To all about, it still doth ring
  A silver chime for me;

For it was placed beside me first,
   Because the word was said—
That none could tell the day or night
   In which I might be dead;
And if I felt my time draw near,
   And had no speech to tell,
'Twas thought I might have strength to ro
   And ring my little Bell.

No wonder that I love to keep
   The Bell within my room,
Which I can never see without
   Preparing for the tomb;
No wonder that its silent voice
   Keeps chiming still for me,—
"You know not, child, the day nor hour
   When I will set you free:"
But no one knows the reason why
   I love and guard so well,
And would not like at all to part
   My little friend—the Bell.

HOPE DEFERRED.

Far, and more far appears the day
   Of my desired repose;
My life seems fainting on its way,
   So sluggishly it goes:
Desires of Thee consume my soul.
When will she touch the longed-for goal?
When shall I reach the blessed shore
Where I can never lose Thee more?

Sad, and more sad appear the hours
   Thus passed away from Thee;
Dark, and more dark the cloud that lowers
   Between my home and me;
The daily faults that, e'er so small,
Still wrong the God who made us all;
The fear of darker sin before
The battle-time of life is o'er.

What wonder, if no thought of good
   To others I impart,
Who cannot love Thee as I would,
   E'en with my own poor heart!
And yet it is such pain to see
Thy creatures turn away from Thee,
Deluded by the world they choose,
And reckless of the God they lose!

When will my weary heart have rest?
   When will its throbbings cease?
When shall I wake upon Thy breast,
   In that sweet world of peace?
O Father! call the pilgrim home,
O Lover! say that longed-for "come,"
O Brother! make me fit to go,
And take me from this world of woe.

DREAMS OF SAINT LEWIS BERTRAND.

With saintly glories full in sight,
   And palms before his eyes,
Saint Lewis left his home by night,
   In holy pilgrim guise;

For in his soul the dream divine
    Was rising night and day,
To visit many a saintly shrine
    In regions far away.

And thus he meant, with staff in hand
    And feet that loved their pain,
To roam through many a foreign land,
    Nor seek his own again;
And, as he turned from home's caress,
    And kindred ties resigned,
He thought how God could trebly bless
    For all he left behind.

A thousand joys came forth to light
    The pilgrim's onward way,
He scanned the starry skies by night,
    The sunny earth by day;
Rejoicing on the wave to look,
    Or kneel upon the sod,
While still, in nature's open book,
    He read the thought of God.

"And, oh!" he said, "this heart shall wake
    To earthly hopes no more,
Alone, in joy for His sweet sake
    To whom its yearnings soar:
From land to land, from clime to clime,
    With trembling speed I'll go,
Nor give my falt'ring soul the time
    To link itself below.

"In lonely cave and grotto blest
    The guardian Saints I'll pray,
New fires to kindle in my breast
    With each succeeding day:

From each I'll learn some secret true
   Which grace divine has wrought,
And every hour, with wonders new,
   Inflame my opening thought.

" Where art has shed her magic grace
   Upon religion's shrine,
I'll seek the influence of the place,
   And share its life divine;
I'll haunt each old Cathedral aisle,
   And hear the booming sound
Of deep-toned voice and organ, while
   The vaulted roofs resound."

Ah! friends, it was a youthful Saint
   For whom such visions rose;
The hand of God doth rarely paint
   In picture-scenes like those!
Soon storms o'ertake his flying feet
   And mock his fairy plan,
And he must turn from dreamings sweet,
   To the rough work of man;

To fight temptation hand to hand,
   To dwell with grief, alone,
To labour in a foreign land
   And suffer in his own:
But, though in no lone cave he lay
   Nor pilgrim traces trod,
He went to Heaven another way,
   And is a Saint with God.

"THE LILY AMONG THORNS."

O Lord! I know thy Lily flower
   With thorns is set about,
Because the bloom of Purity
   Is guarded from without;
And penance, flight, and watchfulness
   Must her true guardians be,
Or else she'll lose the fleckless light
   Which makes her dear to Thee.

But, Lord, from out Thy red Rose flower
   The thorns appear to grow;
'Tis in herself they take their root,—
   And why must this be so?
"Ah! 'tis because red Charity
   Within herself doth bear,
In over-fond solicitude,
   The source of every care.

"The virgin flower of Purity,
   With aspect mild and sweet,
Amid the thorny wilderness
   May bloom in calm retreat;
The royal flower of Charity,
   In care for men below,
And sighs for God above, her own
   Thrice blessèd thorns must grow."

THE LAST COMBAT.

"When I am weak, then I am strong."—2 *Cor.* xii. 10.

When the last hour is close at hand,
And the last foes about me stand,
When the fierce battle hath begun
In which the soul is lost or won,

Who, high o'er angels and o'er men,
Will stand in armour by me then,
And fight my closing battle, free
Of any cost or care to me?
      My Saviour.

When I am lying cold and white,
Scarce fit to pray, much less to fight,
And hell is hissing through the air
Its hideous whispers round me there,
When friends, who weep about my bed,
But little comfort there can shed,
Who'll still my heart with magic sway
And banish all her gloom away?
      My Saviour.

When, knowing that the end is near,
The prince of this world comes in fear
To lose the prey he kept in sight,
And all his rage is at its height,
When every engine he can set
To do his work of ruin yet
Plays fiercely on my parting soul,
Who'll lift her high o'er hell's control?
      My Saviour.

Yes, let me fight Your fight to-day,
While strength is left to work and pray,
And never shrink before the view
Of what You ask my hands to do,
And never care to break the chain
Which You have bound of grief or pain:
But little then I'll stoop to dread
The death-foes closing round my bed,
When all my hope to You hath fled,
And my poor sinking, dying head
Just feels Your arm beneath it spread,
      My Saviour!

MOTHER OF GOD.

How He must have crowned His Mother
 When she entered Heaven above,
All unlike to any other
 Claimant for so dear a love!
He, the God of all creation,
 Owes His human nature still
To the meek and humble Virgin,
 Handmaid of her Master's will.

Never Son was like to Jesus!
 Never child obeyed as He!
Never mother fond as Mary
 Shone in Heaven so gloriously!
Never pangs like those which pierced her
 Mortal bosom dreamed or knew!
Never yet did saint or virgin
 Live so stainless, die so true!

'Tis the loving Child that greets her,
 In the great, eternal Lord;
Still, in His own glorious kingdom,
 Christ obeys His Mother's word.
"I'll deny you nought in Heaven,
 You denied Me nought on earth—"
Read like words that seal her mission,
 And proclaim her priceless worth!

A HYMN FOR OCTOBER.

This is the month of Angels,
 Sing for their love to-day;
Bright are the banded Angels
 Grouping around our way:

These are the sleepless warders,
   These are the keepers mild ;—
Honour the Guardian Angels,
   Woman, and man, and child.

Sing for the grand Archangels,
   Mighty to lead and guide ;
Over the heads that rule us
   They, in their love, preside :
Sing for their holy counsels,
   Sing for their promptings true :
Bending before our rulers,
   Honour their Guardians too.

Sing for the radiant Seven
   Linking the earth and sky ;
First for the great Archangel
   Bearing the standard high ;
Next for the kindly Spirit
   Sent on the work of love ;
Then for the Guide so faithful,
   True to the home above.

Sing for the Princes, bearing
   Light from the founts on high,
Watching the states and kingdoms
   With their unsleeping eye ;
Still, through the din of warfare,
   Doing the work of love,
Drawing the good from all things
   He hath decreed above.

Sing for the guiding Powers :
   They can defeat the wiles
Of the infernal tempter,
   With his deceitful smiles ;

Ever their sword of triumph
    Crosseth his web of ill:
Sing for the holy Powers,
    Fighting our battles still.

Sing for the Virtues, glorious
    In their dominion wide,
Raising the storms and earthquakes
    But to rebuke our pride:
Dread not the vivid lightning,
    Fear not the thunder-call,
Cry to the wondrous Virtues,—
    These are their playthings all.

Sing for the Dominations,
    True to the will divine,
Still, for their Master's glory
    Ever their light doth shine;
Decking the sacred altars,
    Building the churches fair,
Sing for the Dominations,—
    They are your masters there.

Sing for the Thrones, reposing
    In their secure abode,
These are the peaceful Angels,
    Making the seat of God:
Never a shade disturbing
    Crosses their sacred sphere;
Ask of the Thrones unceasing
    Share of their spirit here.

Sing for the Cherubs, blazing
    With their mysterious light,
Piercing the awful secrets,
    Hid in the Infinite:

Theirs is the gift of wisdom,
   And they delight to shine
Bright on the lowly spirit,
   Keeping the law divine.

Sing for the Seraphs burning,
   Lost in the flame of love,
Drinking in heavenly secrets,
   Clasping their God above:
This is their circling glory,
   This is their crowning ray,—
Still, to love on for ever
   Just as they love to-day.

Sing for the Queen of Angels,—
   These are her victor bands;
Still are their bright ranks waving
   Just as her eye commands;
Still are their glad gifts waking,
   Ready to meet her call:
Sing for the Virgin Mary,
   Queen of the Angels all.

Sing for the God who made them—
   Angels and Queen above,
Sing for the God who gave them
   From His great Heart of love:
Still may that love consume us
   With its sweet ardours here,
Till we go forth as Angels,
   Fit for His own bright sphere.

BEADS FROM THE HOLY SEPULCHRE.

My Lord! it was a tender thought of my sick-room and me
Which brought this hallowed Rosary far over land and sea:
The pilgrim-bearer little knew for whom the beads were meant,—
From Thee and from Thy loving Heart the sacred gift was sent.

Thrice blest, upon Thy Tomb it hung, and 'twas for this alone
Thou didst inspire a friendly hand to place it in mine own;
For soon, as on my heart it lay, I fast began to prove
How every bead was teeming o'er with token-words of love.

It spoke of all Thy wanderings, it told of all Thy tears,
Thy shame and pain and agony, Thy weariness and fears;
It asked, with thrilling tenderness, if greater love could be
Than this which brought my Saviour down to the cold Tomb for me.

And then my thoughts rushed onward, and questioned if it came
Because this faster-beating heart and more exhausted frame
Are but of my own early grave a token and a sign,
Which I could meet more tranquilly for this kind glance from Thine.

Oh! be it word of life or death, to Thee my soul I lift,
In thanks for all the tenderness which breathes from out Thy gift:
And still, at every bead, I pray for blessings on the hand
Which placed in mine the Rosary from the far, Holy Land.

FINAL PERSEVERANCE.

   Lord! my hope shall never waver
   For that last and highest favour,—
From this life in peace to part:
   So to live in constant trying,
   That I'll die in ardent sighing
For a place within Your Heart.

   By that Blood which flowed to save me,
   By each proof of love You gave me,
This last dearest grace impart:
   By the tears of Mary weeping,
   Near the cross her vigil keeping,
Bid her place me in Your Heart.

HOMEWARD BOUND.

"True love is worship;"—evermore
   To this our hearts are moving:
And, with their instinct to adore,
   Brook no restraint in loving:
Before Thy works they fain would kneel,—
   To *Thee* too seldom kneeling,
And, with intense desire to feel,
   Scarce heed what they are feeling.

But, blessed hour of truth and light!
   When idols fall before Thee,
And each heart owns her inborn right
   To love and to adore Thee;
When rapt, and filled before Thy Shrine,
   She fears no just reproving,
For hearts that beat with love divine
   Need set no bounds to loving.

DISAPPOINTMENT.

O Lord! how often is the cup
To my parched lips held, brimming up,
Whose welcome draught would ease my pain,—
But, as I stoop, 'tis gone again.

O Lord! how often do I see
The friendly archer aim at me,
But while I seem to fix his eye—
Alas! his dart has passed me by!

O Lord! how often do I stand
In sight of that mysterious land,
Which to my constant thought doth wear
A home-like and familiar air;

But, as my bark goes lightly o'er,
And I have all but touched the shore,
A sudden gale is sure to rise,
Which blows me back to these dull skies.

Yet, Lord! 'tis sweet to think, at last
Such disappointments must be past,—
That if I make of Death a friend,
I can't be cheated in the end.

SAINT SEBASTIAN.

Bound naked to the pillar,
   Thy meek eyes raised above,
With a look in which thine anguish
   Is mingling with thy love,
Thy flesh in keenest torture,
   As the piercing arrows play,
Thy hands all bound and helpless,
   As thy life-blood ebbs away!

Oh, martyred Saint Sebastian!
   What lesson can I trace
In the sharpness of thy torment,
   And the patience of thy face!
And I say unto my spirit,
   "Thus stripped naked must thou stay,
While the darts of fierce temptation
   Round thy silent anguish play."

Oh, faithful Saint Sebastian!
   The arrows long ago
Have ceased their work of torture,
   And the crown is on thy brow;
Thine eyes are raised as ever
   In the fulness of their love,
But their pain hath changed to triumph
   In the glorious courts above.

And thus, if I should conquer
   Through the combats that remain
With the loneliness of sorrow
   And the arrow-darts of pain,

My struggles will be over
   And my labours will be done,
And I'll wear the crown of victor
   For the battles I have won.

Oh, patient Saint Sebastian!
   Since thy martyrdom doth rise
For ever, as a figure
   Of mine own, before mine eyes,
Wilt thou cheer me in the sorrow,
   Wilt thou aid me in the strife,
Till I pass unto my Saviour
   Through the martyrdom of life.

MY TIMES ARE IN THY HAND.

No more I pray to pass away
   Ere pain shall come to try me,—
Such prayer to die was but to fly
   From sign of battle nigh me.

Thy standard raise before my gaze,
   No more I fear to view it;
If Thou wilt stay to show the way,
   I'll prove my fealty to it.

What care have I to live or die,
   To suffer or rejoice,
So I but tread where Thou hast led,
   And hearken to Thy voice?

When Thou dost know me fit to go,
   Thou'lt not be slow to take me;
And while I stand at Thy command,
   Far less wilt Thou forsake me.

I only pray, while here I stay,
  That Thou wilt stay beside me
To shade the light which shines too bright,
  And through the darkness guide me.

PRAYER.

Oh, for a quiet hour with Thee,
  My heart to Thy Heart given,
Thy still delights pervading me,
  Till earth seems changed to Heaven!
Oh, for a silent hour of prayer,
  Thyself alone to hear me,
And not a thought of worldly care
  To cast its shadow near me!

Oh, for the hour when prayer will be
  My spirit's whole employment,
And undivided love to Thee
  Her sweet and sole enjoyment!
Oh, for the hour of death, to send
  Such free and full communion!
Oh, for the hours of prayer which tend
  To this eternal union!

MARY IS OUR QUEEN.

How fast, at Mary's first command,
  The Angel bands are seen
To work her will by sea and land,
  For Mary is their Queen!

And well they pay their debt of love,
    And pleased they are to know—
This Queen, whom they obey above,
    Their God obeyed below.

        The Angel bands, the Angel bands,
            How fast they may be seen
        To wing their flight as she commands,—
            For Mary is their Queen!

Oh, high o'er every Angel choir
    Is Mary's seat of love!
And sweet the sound of Mary's lyre
    The Angel harps above!
And glad the Angels are to go
    Where Mary's mandates call,
And hear her voice, because they know
    She loves above them all.

        The Angel choirs, the Angel choirs,
            How swift they may be seen
        To move as Mary's heart desires,—
            For Mary is their Queen!

Now let us learn on earth to live
    As Angels live above,
And still new proofs of homage give
    To this great Queen of love:
For, right through Mary's heart the way
    To Christ's dear Heart is found,
And they who Mary's word obey,
    By Mary's Son are crowned.

        Dear Angel choirs, dear Angel choirs,
            May we, like you, be seen
        To live as Mary's heart desires,—
            For Mary is our Queen!

WHITE LILIES.

Six stamens hath the Lily flower,
   On which six anthers glow:
On six degrees of Purity
   Six crowns doth God bestow.

And first, the blessed Angels speak
   Unto the pure in heart,
And many a holy secret there
   Familiarly impart.

And next, the God of purity
   Draws nigh unto the pure,
For they have won Him down to them
   By such a potent lure.

The chaste espousals follow fast,
   In which the Lamb doth love
And crown the soul who rates such bliss
   All earthly ties above.

Then, grow the spirit-children up,—
   Souls saved, and good works done,
And virgin emulation fired
   By crowns the pure have won.

Beyond, are high prerogatives:
   For they who could despise
The lowliness of nature,
   To the heights of grace should rise.

But still, their fullest recompense
   Is wrought for them above,
Where they alone shall follow
   In the track of Him they love.

THE PARTICULAR JUDGMENT.

Oh! when wilt Thou free me?
Oh! when shall I see Thee?
Oh! when will that rapturous moment draw near
When my bonds shall be broken,
My sentence be spoken
By lips that I worship too fondly to fear?

With sighs to be near Thee,
To see and to hear Thee,
With watching and waiting and yearning for Thee,
With burning to meet Thee,
To bless and to greet Thee—
I scarcely demand what Thy sentence will be.

Oh! what shall o'er-awe me,
Where all seem to draw me,—
Thy judgments, Thy mercies, Thy justice, Thy love?
Thy grandeur delights me
Where most it affrights me—
A Saviour beside me, a Monarch above!

Oh! when shall I see Thee?
Oh! when wilt Thou free me?
Ah! how canst Thou leave me to languish and sigh?—
When my bonds might be broken,
My welcome outspoken,
And Heaven come to meet me, if once I could die!

EXTREME UNCTION.

Oh! sweet and pitying Sacrament
Which gives the grace to die,
Did ever any need so much,
Or love thee more than I?

For, my impatient soul desires
  Too much her lot to choose,
And hoping soon to see her God,
  She dreads that hope to lose;
But, at thy consecrating touch,
  From many a stain set free,
She'll settle to a calmer trust
  In that which is to be.

Oh, sweet and healing Sacrament!
  If thou art come for life,
Thrice welcome be the will of God,
  And earth's continued strife:
With every sense impressed by God,
  I'll strive to bear in mind
That Holy Oils should hallow still
  The spot which they have signed:
I'll keep His counsels in my heart,
  And ever more I'll be
Preparing, through my life, to meet
  The stroke that sets me free.

But, sweet and smiling Sacrament!
  If thou art come to-day
To say my hopes will soon be crowned,
  My sorrows pass away,
Oh! still through all, let me preserve
  My faith and promise true—
To love, because it pleases God,
  What pleases nature too;
Then, when His time is come at last
  To set my spirit free,
Die, whispering to my gentle God,
  " 'Tis all for love of Thee."

SNOW-WREATHS.

Down on the ground the white snow lay,
Reminding me of that blest day
When Saint Teresa's priests could steal
From out the cloister's shade, to kneel
And pray, in cold and piercing air,
The snow-shower falling round them there,
Yet never feel its icy touch,
The burning of their hearts was such!

Down on the ground the snow-flakes white
Remind me of that holy night
On which Saint Francis, wandering late,
Knocked vainly at his convent gate,
And then for hours exulting knelt
Rejoicing in each pang he felt,
Because he knew *whose* Hand had flung
The snow which to his thin robe clung.

Down on the ground the snow-hues faint
Remind me of that crownèd Saint*
Who rose by night to seek the shrine;
And, in the warmth of love divine,
Bade his benumbed attendant take
The pathway which *his* steps should make,
As he had felt the frozen sod
Grow warm beneath him where he trod.

Down on the ground the untrodden snow
Reminds me of that virgin brow,†
Which, pure in life and pure in death,
Looked lovelier for its martyr-wreath;
And, sacred to the God on high,
Was hid from every blighting eye,
And shrined in virgin bloom below,
By sudden shower of falling snow.

* Saint Wenceslaus. † Saint Eulalia.

Down on the ground the snow-wreaths there
Remind me of the piercing air,
While Mary vainly strove to warm
Her new-born Infant's trembling form ;
Or clasped Him in her arms so tight,
To shield Him from the blast that night
When Joseph sadly bade her fly,
Lest morn should see the Infant die.

Down on the ground the snowy spray
Reminds me of Christ's poor to-day,
Who keep the footway of their God,
And tread e'en as the saints have trod.
Oh! hear us, Saviour, while we pray
To love these saints of our own day,
And gladly labour and endure,
To serve Thee in Thy suffering poor.

A PREMIUM FOR SILENCE.

Upon gold-strung lyres do the Angels play
  And sing to their God on high,
And many an echo doth hitherward stray
  From the far off Land in the sky.

But the wheels of the world go busily round,
  And labour and strife and mirth
Will seldom let anyone hear the sound
  Of the angel-harps on earth.

But he who would keep himself hushed and still,
  From the revel and din apart,
And, doing his work with an upright will,
  Would quietly pray in his heart,

While the wheels of the world go dizzily round,
    And pageant and throng sweep by,
Would hear in his spirit the echoing sound
    Of the angel-harps on high.

THE LASTING TREASURE.

"Where your treasure is, there will your heart be also."—*Luke*, xii. 34.

When dying, oh! what should my agony be
If I were found clinging to any but Thee!
However I held it, my grasp could not stay,
And my soul would shriek wildly in hastening away.

Oh! what can secure me when that will befall,
But loving Thee only, and loving Thee all?
Thou wilt not reject, though unworthy I be—
Thou wilt not cast off who has no one but Thee!

For this dost Thou leave me so long upon earth,
That free and unfettered, I yet may go forth;
Each hour of my exile is filing the chain,—
Till the last links are severed, 'tis well to remain.

My soul, for His call let us patiently wait,
And never for Him let our efforts abate;
Use life for the ends for which life has been given,
Hail death as the long wished-for passport to Heaven.

OUR LADY OF THE SACRED HEART.

Our Lady of the Sacred Heart!
  Unlock thy stores to-day,
And from those mines of grace impart
  That gift for which I pray:
Thou knowest the heavy burdens laid
  On weary mind and frame;
Thou knowest how long I've wept and prayed,
  Yet suffered still the same.

Thou knowest, I did not seek thy face
  For comfort or for cure,
So much as for sustaining grace
  To combat and endure:
While patience strengthened with distress,
  While prayer seemed born of pain
I did not ask to suffer less,
  Nor wear a lighter chain;

But now, beneath a crushing load
  I have no strength to bear,
I seem to totter on the road
  Of patience and of prayer.
Then, Lady of the Sacred Heart!
  Stretch out thy hand to me;
The God of every healing art
  Works all His cures through thee.

BLESSINGS.

How lonely would my life appear,
  If blessings did not grow
And mingle with the atmosphere
  About me, as I go!

I know not how the prayer is heard
  Which dies within the air,
Almost before I catch the word
  That tells me it is there,—
But still my foot doth lighter tread,
  My heart more gladly beat,
Whene'er I hear "God bless you" said
  Behind me in the street;
And when I lead the blind along,
  Or show a child the way,
The blessing I so cheaply win
  Can cheer me through the day.

How lonesomely I'd pass my days,
  If holy Church should cease
To bless me, in a thousand ways
  Of kindness and of peace!
The Holy Water by my bed,
  The Palm within my sight,
The Beads on which her hand hath shed
  Such mystery and might!
When priestly hands are raised on high
  Above my prostrate soul,
Their power to heal and purify,
  To quiet and console!
The blessings murmured at the close
  Of Mass and Sermon too—
Oh! he who feels them only knows
  What mighty work they do!

Then, let them rain upon my way
  And grow about my feet,
From children pausing at their play
  Or beggars in the street;

From strangers that I chance to see
   And aid, in passing by,
From friends whose comfort I may be
   When sickness comes to try;
From Medals, with their sacred touch,
   And Holy Water kind,—
I cannot value overmuch
   What Mother Church hath signed:
And what if thickening graces fall
   Around me all the day!
'Tis wandering blessings seem to call
   Them down upon my way.

SOLACE FOR THE WEAK.

Who knows if You have not removed
   My health and strength from me,
Lest evil snares they both had proved
   For my weak soul to be?
I might have done great works on earth,
   And died as many do—
A toiler almost from my birth—
   Yet done no work for You!

I might have shared in many a scene
   Of action and of strife,
And won there many a garland green
   To deck my day of life;
I might have been a "runner fast,"
   And crowned a victor too
To find, when on my death-bed cast,
   I had not run towards You.

Who knows how far the darkened room,
    The lengthened hours of pain,
The frequent warnings from the tomb
    Have been a wholesome chain—
To bind a faithless nature down,
    To save from deeds untrue,
To guard for an eternal crown
    What else were lost to You!

THE WINGS OF MY ANGEL.

Dear Wings of my Angel! spread over my way
To guard and to shelter my soul when I pray!
Dear Wings of my Angel! extended at night,
Lest the spirit of evil should hurt or affright!

Dear Wings of my Angel! unfolded again
When my forehead is throbbing with fever and pain!
Which fan me and cool me, and bear from above
The healing of pity, the balsam of love!

Dear Wings of my Angel! whose flutterings clear
Make a wonderful music, most charming to hear,
Which weave, while you circle, the airs I love best,
Bringing songs to my waking and dreams to my
    rest!

Dear Wings of my Angel! which glitter and glow
With a thousand bright glories as onward I go,
Which shed from your white plumes a fragrance in
    air,
To which earth's sweetest odours have nought to
    compare!

Dear Wings of my Angel! oh! ne'er may I take
Affright at the shadow you sometimes can make,
But own that the ray which you hide from my sight
Would but lure to the regions of horror and night.

Dear Wings of my Angel! I love you as well
As the bird loves its nest or the hermit his cell;
All earth were a snare, and all life were a fear
If my God had not taught me to save myself here.

BLESSED MARIA BARTHOLOMÆA.

Blessed Maria, Virgin of the Order of Saint Dominic, on being urged by her father to marry, was seized with a mysterious distemper, which rendered her life, for forty-five years, a martyrdom of suffering. (Died, 1577.)

LITTLE of thy life I know,
   But it comforts me to hear
That such lengthened pangs below
   Won a crown so high and dear:
When I think how sickness pressed
   On thy young life year by year,
I can trace out all the rest
   For my own instruction here.

Though thy features looked so still
   And thine accents spoke so kind,
Nature did not fail to thrill,
   Grace it was that felt resigned:
When thy pangs too rudely rent,
   Prayer was all in all to thee;
Can I doubt, if there I leant,
   Prayer would be the same to me?

I can see thee looking back
    To thy sisters, as they passed
Through a wild and desert track,
    To their promised Land at last:
If their pains were strength to thee,
    Didst thou ask their prayers above,—
Thou wilt kindly look on me
    Claiming too, a sister's love.

It is said the name of *sin*
    Caused such anguish in thy heart
That the room it beat within
    In thy tremblings bore a part:
May my heart this anguish drink
    Till it flee from every snare,
And, in sorrow, only think
    How to make atonement there.

I am told that all the day,
    Fast by iron sickness bound,
'Twas thy dear delight to pray
    For the slumb'ring souls around;
Till thy patience and thy pain,
    Crying to the ear of love,
Snapped asunder many a chain
    Which the power of hell had wove.

Were I patient, too, and meek,
    Mine would not be useless years;
God has pity on the weak,
    And would hear me for my tears.
Oh, my sister, most of all
    'Tis thy burning zeal I crave;
May my fetters break the thrall
    Of the souls He died to save!

WORK FOR SAINT PATRICK.

So many sainted shall I sing,
    And find no lay for thee
Who wast the saint of saints to bring
    God's first, best gift to me?—
To me, and to my native land,
    Where faith lit up to blaze
More brightly 'neath each daring hand
    That strove to quench its rays.

Oh, always loved, if never sung!
    Accept the feeble lay
Which seems to falter on the tongue
    Where words must fail to-day;
Some other hour the tide will flow,
    The waters gush forth free,
And I shall pay the debt I owe
    To holy Church and thee:

But now a secret sorrow weighs
    Upon my spirit's wing,
And when I seek the note of praise,
    The note of woe I sing;
For while the faith by Patrick taught,
    The hopes by Patrick sown
Are through our inmost life inwrought,
    Our glory and our crown,

We desecrate the land he trod,
    And wring his heart with shame
By flinging in the face of God
    A sin I need not name!

O brethren, who to faith can yield
    A homage high and due,
Yet God's own image will not shield,
    But blot it out of view!

Who, for a short and base delight,
    Will, at some grovelling feast,
Before your great Creator's sight
    From man sink down to beast!
O Patrick! who hath heart for song
    That still such sights must see?
God grant it be not overlong
    Till they are passed from me!

MUSIC WORTH WAITING FOR.

O lovers of music, consider
    What rapturous sounds you will hear
When Angels are harping around you
    And warbling their melodies dear!
Oh! these are the song-birds of Heaven,—
    But Mary's sweet cadences fall
And rise, like the nightingale's singing,
    A thousand times sweeter than all.

Oh! glad are the lips of our Mother
    In praising the God of her love,
In leading the chant of the virgins
    Who sing the new carol above!
When Mary is singing the anthem,
    The chorus by saints chanted near,
With all the glad echoes resounding—
    Oh! blest are the ears that shall hear!

O lovers of music, consider
    If 'twould not be well to resign
Such songs as might lure you to losing
    All right in the music divine;
The songs of the earth will be over,—
    Alas! if they tempt you to rove
From such as are always beginning
    Afresh in the kingdom of love!

HOME.

Home! home! Still the cry pierceth upwards to Thee!
I pine in my fetters,—I long to be free;
I've nothing to cling to, and nowhere to stay,—
Oh! why must I linger thus, day after day?

Home! home! Of what use is my life to Thee here?
A creature of sorrow and weakness and fear,
With tears ever falling for sin or for woe,
Like a shade on the daylight, I linger below.

Home! home! There my spirit would mount on the wing!
Oh, how lightly I'd laugh and how sweetly I'd sing,
And I'd pray, with Thy sainted, rejoicing to be
A buckler for all I left fighting for Thee.

Home! home! In my anguish I cry to Thee still,
Yet I trust in Thy mercy and wait on Thy will;
The cry must be uttered, the tears must have way,
But my home is Thy Providence day after day.

THE PRESENTATION NUN.

I LIKE to sit and think about
    The Presentation Nun,
Her life so little known or praised,
    Her labours never done;
It rarely comes her way to hear
    A word which seems to prove
That she is recognised on earth
    As one who works for love.

Men do not see her good works shine,
    And scruple not to say
Her talent, hid within the earth,
    Can only rust away;
They twit her with her idle prayers,
    And show the service true
That, to the sick and maimed and poor,
    Saint Vincent's daughters do.

Long may Saint Vincent's daughters walk
    Like angels, through the land,
And read a lesson to the world
    It needs must understand;
But no more gracious mission yet
    Hath minstrel ever sung
Than that with which her God doth charge
    The Presentation Nun.

No time she finds to reap on earth,
    So constantly she sows;
She watches still the dawn of life,
    Let others watch its close!

Her work is with the youthful mind,
    Her place is in the school,
Her whole perfection twined about
    The one, unvarying rule.

Though seldom does the eye of man
    Upon her work look down,
Yet not the less does God behold
    The labours He will crown;
Nor ever turns His glance aside,
    Nor less reward will pay
Because His roughest work is done
    To-morrow as to-day.

For God it is no task to watch
    The ever-shifting throng,
To track each individual life
    From out the school-house gone:
He crowns the hardy battles fought
    In black temptation's strife,
He leads the weeping wanderers back
    To the fresh springs of life;

And for the saints that He has kept,
    The sinners He has won,
He has His chosen day to thank
    The Presentation Nun,
Who vows her life to labours here,
    Unheeded as His own,
And, when His harvest-time has come
    Will reap what she hath sown.

CHARITAS.

I am come to cast fire on the earth."—Luke, xii. 49.

Love! love! How fast the cry ascends
   To Thy eternal throne!
A mighty rush is in its wings
   Which bear to Thee alone;
By night and day that one demand
   The yearning heart sends forth,—
Love! love! Didst Thou not come to cast
   Its flame upon the earth?

Love! love! See how it smiles upon
   Pain, poverty, and shame,
The sacred three that fuel bring
   To feed its ardent flame!
How hell falls back in wild dismay
   To see it leap and soar,
As fierce temptation makes it blaze
   Still brighter than before!

Love! love! If love and bliss were found
   Apart on Heaven's own shore,
We'd take the love, and let the bliss
   Be lost for evermore;
Why then on earth affrighted be,
   Because, our faith to try,
The road of love and pain awhile
   Together seem to lie?

Love! love! Oh, let the cry ascend
   For ever to Thy throne!
And ever give our yearning hearts
   An answer from Thine own;

And come again, and oft again,
    With hands that cannot tire
To kindle in our earthy souls
    Thy all-consuming fire.

A LEGEND OF MELLERAYE.

THERE is a lone chapel all tranquil and blest,
And stately the sentinels guarding its rest;
For no city beholds it, no village is nigh,
But it springs from the mountains right under the sky;
With the free winds around it, its foot on the sod,
And its face looking up to the blue eye of God,
With its banner of piety sweetly unfurled,
And hid, like a nun, from the gaze of the world.

Ah! once on the Sabbath-day lingering there,
I heard the low vesper-bell calling to prayer,
And bowed down adoring, while grandly the sound
Of the mellow-toned organ came winding around;
While a peace and a rapture I could not control,
Like a breathing from Heaven, came into my soul;
And I thought if God called me to dwell with Him there,
How gladly I'd serve Him in labour and prayer.

Now the vespers are passed and the feeling is o'er,
And mine eyes may behold the lone chapel no more;
But I love to remember the beam o'er its face,
Like the blessing of God on that desolate place,

To hush my wild heart with the memories dear
That twine round that vesper-bell tinkling and clear;
And, though far from the mountain-church, still
    would I glean
And sing every legend that's linked with the scene:

    The setting sun fell grand and fair
      Upon the mountain's breast,
    When, full of labour, peace, and prayer,
      The monks lay down to rest.
    Short hours of slumber! soon to cease,
      But felt and prized the more
    For shadowing forth the heavenly peace
      When all life's toils are o'er.

    And calmly fell the evening ray
      Upon their foreheads bare,
    And calm the sainted brethren lay
      As if they slept in prayer;
    Or if a smile unconscious stole
      Upon some sleeping face,
    'Twas dream of Heaven that sought a soul
      So full of heavenly grace.

    But one, with brow contract and stern,
      Seems wrung with sudden pain;—
    Perchance his thoughts have yet to learn
      The peace of holy men;
    Perchance the countless links that bind
      Each human heart below
    For mastery o'er the sleepless mind
      Are striving wildly now!

    God comfort him! if he have come
      To that lone mountain's breast,
    And found within his convent home
      But sadness and unrest:

God aid him! if he turn away
  With many a vain regret,
And shrink from every weary day
  That must await him yet!

But God's good Angels hovering there
  Could tell another tale
Of what has knit that forehead bare,
  And worn that cheek so pale.
Oh! he may toil like fettered slave,
  And pray with seraph fire,—
One sinner's soul he cannot save
  From God's avenging fire!

He had a brother in his youth,
  Dearer than aught but Heaven,
And still, against God's light and truth,
  That brother's soul had striven;
Till he had left him drunk with wrong,
  When, to that mount ascending,
He knelt amid that cowlèd throng
  In prayer for the offending.

Oh! how his sad life wore away
  In toil and prayer and sorrow,
And still the grief of every day
  Was fresh upon the morrow;
And still his waking sighs were shed
  In painful dreams whenever
He sank upon that weary bed
  Where his *heart* rested—never.

*   *   *   *

The mild rays of the autumn moon
  Fell on the mountain's breast,—
A brother's soul will pass full soon
  To its eternal rest:

The holy hymns are chanted there,
    The holy lustre shed,
The abbot kneels in peaceful prayer
    Beside the dying bed.

"My father, one disturbing thought
    Haunts me with vain regret,—
Another's grace from Heaven I sought,
    And have not found it yet.
I had a brother, young and dear,
    But guilty, proud, and gay,—
Pray God would guide his footsteps here
    Before his dying day!

"Pray, father, with a ceaseless prayer,
    A vigil never done;
One human soul is worth the care
    Of God's eternal Son.
Dark was my life with constant thought
    Though *I* in Heaven might dwell,
How black the cup, with anguish fraught,
    Which *he* must drink in hell!
But now I look to Heaven above
    And half forget my cares,
Commending him to God's sweet love
    And your most holy prayers."

"Lift up thine eyes," the abbot said:
    He gazed enraptured there;
For, e'en beside his dying bed
    That lost one bent in prayer.
No clasping now of kindred hand,
    No close and dear embrace,—
Enough to see the pardoned stand
    In God's redeeming grace.
What now, the thrilling pain and fear,
    The vigil long and dim?

Oh how he blesses every tear
  That he has wept for him!
Yes, o'er that brother he had sighed
  With sighs that would not cease,
While he, reclaimed and purified,
  Knelt by his side in peace.

NIGHT-THOUGHTS.

I AM locked within my cell,
  And my heart is free
Once again in peace to dwell
  With her thoughts of Thee:
Darkly as within my room
  Night's own shadows glide,
Still they cast not half the gloom
  Of the world outside.

Death is to my thought, when here,
  Present evermore;
To forget his face I fear
  On life's restless shore.
Here I live for only Thee,—
  When abroad I move,
Many a phantom wileth me
  From Thy constant love.

Once when sickness came I said—
  "Let me rise again,
For I burn Thy light to shed
  On the hearts of men."
Now I pray, "Let *saints* go forth
  To life's stormy din!—
Hide *me* in some spot of earth
  Where I may not sin."

O my God! I cannot bear
    Life which wars with Thee:
Health and joy seem but a snare
    Spread abroad for me;
In the fear lest I offend
    Scarce I dare to please;—
When some respite wilt Thou send
    From such fears as these?

MY PRAYER TO SAINT DOMINIC.

FATHER dear, with humble prayer
    To thy shrine I flee,
A daughter's love to offer there,
    All worthless though it be.
Father, guide me to the last
    With paternal heart;
Hold me firm and bind me fast,
    And never say—depart.

Thy white tunic may I bear
    Without stain or spot,
Thy dark robe of penance wear
    And disgrace it not:
Crownèd saints so linked with me!—
    Oh! the crying shame
If their sister I should be,
    Less in deed than name!

Father, pour thy spirit in
    Through this soul of mine,
Till the heaven-taught faith within
    Lives and glows like thine:

On my forehead set the seal
   Still thine own to be;
Fill me with the burning zeal
   Which o'erflowed in thee.

Father, teach me how to claim
   Mary's love my own;
Bid me seek her in Thy name,
   Lead me to her throne:
Ask Saint Magdalen to pray
   For thy child in Heaven,
Till the Saviour's lips shall say—
   " Love, and be forgiven."

Father dear, with homage true
   To thy shrine I flee,
To offer in thy kindly view
   A daughter's love to thee;
By the holy name I bear
   And the love I feel,
Hear my vow, accept my prayer,
   And bless me where I kneel.

OUR CONSTANT COMPANIONS.

Those numberless Angels that circle and play—
Round the earth, through the heavens, by night and
   by day,
That soothe us when weary, that aid us when weak,
That prompt what we wish for, and bring what we
   seek!

Those mystical Angels that sing to our souls,
That teach us life's meaning, as onward it rolls,
That wrest us from danger, that woo us to right,
That watch while we slumber, and nerve when we fight!

Those wonderful Angels whose love is so true!
They never seem weary whatever we do;
They guard to the latest, they cling to the last,
Give aid to the present to bury the past.

And yet, loving Angels, how little we care
For the wealth that you lavish, the love that you bear!
A thought at our rising, a word ere we sleep
Are our thanks for a love-watch so tender and deep!

Oh! shine on our darkness, and teach us to know
That bright Spirits track us wherever we go,
That sweeter companions than earth ever gave
Pursue like a lover, and serve like a slave.

O Lord of the Angels! who bade them go forth
With radiance of Heaven to light up the earth!
How far wilt Thou bear it, how long wilt Thou view
The sinner so thankless, the Angel so true?

LOVE'S YEARNINGS.

"Who will give me wings like a dove."—Ps. liv. 7.

Who will give me the nightingale's voice
  To sing to my true Love all day?
Who will give me the wings of the turtle
  To fly to my true Love away?

Oh! one or the other petition
  My heart is still hovering near,
For fain would I see Him in Heaven,
  And fain would I sing for Him here.

Who will give me the spirit so tender,
  That thrills to the pleasure alone
And waits for the will of her true Love,
  Before she is sure of her own?
Who will give me the life that is dying
  To sin and to self evermore?
Who will give me the death that upbeareth
  To all that I love and adore?

MEETING SAINT ALPHONSUS IN HEAVEN.

Courage at thy very name
Kindles through my soul and frame;
Just to see it written down
Is to me like palm and crown.

I can think and I can dare,
I can breathe the freest air,
I can trample pain and fear
When 'tis whispered in mine ear.

If I heard and if I saw,
Scarcely closer could I draw;
Had'st thou pledged thyself to me,
Scarcely could I surer be.

When I go to Heaven on high,
I shall know thee in the sky;
I shall know thee from them all,
At thy feet in homage fall;

Kiss these feet whose traces shower
Still to me the forward road,
Bless those hands whose labours here
Made my way to Heaven so clear;

Glance one moment on that brow
Which no grief can shadow now;
Hail thee, once and always free
From each pang I've wept for thee:

Then, rememb'ring where we meet,
Go with thee to Mary's feet,
And before her Saviour Son,
Tell thee that thy task is done.

VARIETIES.

How easily and tenderly
  Do saintly hands entwine
Some charm of holy sentiment
  To blossom round the shrine!
Their prayer is oft in poesy,
  And many a shifting light
Of sunny fancy plays upon
  Their virtue's lofty height;

For love is still the lighting up
  And radiance of the soul,
And all her hues look brighter
  In His merciful control:
He smiles upon the flowers
  While He feeds upon the fruit;
And though oft He prunes the branches,
  Yet He likes to see them shoot.

Saint Francis, in the far-off land,
   Upon his heart enshrined
The name of Saint Ignatius in
   A reliquary twined;
Nor would he wait for death to crown
   And canonize above
The living Saint who nurtured him
   In wisdom and in love.

Saint Bernard sent, with care and cost,
   To claim the body back
Of some poor monk who died upon
   His missionary track,
Because he could not bear to think
   How, desolate and lone,
The stranger earth would cover him,
   And shut him from his own.

The pure and holy Nicholas
   Could never feel at rest
In presence of Saint Lewis till
   His faults had been confessed;
For, in his friend, he reverenced
   A Saint of the Most High,
And feared to meet, unpurified,
   His penetrating eye.

Our own Saint Catherine, when called
   "My daughter" by the Lord,
With such a strong, interior joy
   Exulted at the word,
That she besought her confessor
   To name her so again,
That so the kindling memory
   Might waken for her then.

Saint Rose had her tall rosemaries
    She never wished to part,
Because, like crosses, they grew up,
    While preaching to her heart;
And, if she gave, they pined until
    She claimed them back once more,
When soon, beneath her ardent eyes,
    They flourished as before.

Saint Jane brought many a smiling flower
    Upon the shrine to lie,
In sight of the Omnipotent,
    To fade away and die;
But, after their sweet martyrdom,
    Again her treasures sought,
That through their hallowing neighbourhood
    Heart-wonders might be wrought.

Oh! is there any tracking out
    The ways through which they strike?—
These Saints, so widely different,
    And yet so very like!
For still, through all variety,
    What Saint was ever found
Unguarded by humility,
    By charity uncrowned?

"QUEEN OF ALL SAINTS."

CREATED as none else have been,
    Outshining far the best!
In thee are all perfections seen
    More perfectly possessed;

The martyrs yield their palms surpassed,
    The virgins seek thy throne
Their lilies at thy feet to cast,
    For none are like thine own.

To confessors, their richest years
    Seem light before thy shrine;
The penitents might lose their tears
    In the great sea of thine;

The hermits watch thine eagle gaze
    Rejoicing in the Sun,
And, much as they have loved His rays,
    They own themselves outdone.

By every gift of highest grace
    And charm of purest love,
Sweet Mary, dost thou hold thy place
    As " Queen of Saints" above!

UPLAND.

So many Saints in Heaven that I am sure to know!
So many loving Angels to greet me as I go!
The Mother's smile to welcome, the Father's word to cheer,
The Spouse to whom my lone heart turns from its dark exile here!
No wonder I am longing—no wonder that I pine,
With weary heart and aching brow, for that sweet home of mine!
With thinking of the glorious forms that wander to and fro,
I'm getting more at home in Heaven than on this earth below.

I feel so like a stranger in this world's glare and gaze,
I seem to have forgotten that I ever trod its ways;
They never guess of what I think, nor speak of what I love—
The dear old names of Heaven, the "Household Words" above.
Or let their talk be holy, 'tis in a foreign tongue—
They speak by rule and measure, and breathe when they are done!
I miss the blessed freedom, the heart-breath quick and fond—
Their life is all around them, and *mine* is all beyond.

If 'twere not for my Angel who still His face can see,
And for His own true Presence here, though all unseen by me,
And for the blessed power of prayer upon His aid to call,
I think that in this weary world I could not live at all.
O Father! won't you take me? O Mother! won't you say
You want your own poor child in Heaven without this long delay?
O Saints, that watch above me, and Angels standing by,
What makes me so unfit to live, if I am not to die?

FORESHADOWING.

Teach me the art of holy sighs,
   While here upon Thy Heart I rest;
And give such tears unto mine eyes
   As feed love's flame within the breast—
Such peaceful tears as sweetly stream
   Because the heart is overfraught
With love and joy, and does not seem
   To thank or worship as it ought.

Oh! sweet it is to rest with Thee,
   The voices of the tempest o'er,
And feel Thy breathings kind and free,
   Where fierce temptation howled before:
What were it then, in that blest land
   Where threatening demons dare not come.
Beneath Thy kindling gaze to stand
   And hear Thy joyful welcome home!

WELCOME HOME.

Wilt Thou come on a sudden, "a thief in the night,"
   To her who is watching by night and by day,
Who thirsts for that moment of love and delight
   When the voice of the Bridegroom will summon away?
Wilt Thou find her in slumber whose heart cannot rest
   Lest ever its beatings should cease to be Thine?
Shall Thy darts have a pang for that penitent breast
   Which asks but to suffer and bleed at Thy shrine?

Sweet Jesus! *my* Victim! accept me as Thine;
  So bind in Thy fetters as ne'er to set free,
Nor let my frail spirit one moment decline
  From her faith, or her hope, or her yearnings for Thee.
Keep such ardours for ever alive in my heart
  That, by night or by day, she can answer—"I come!"
And in the same moment which sees me depart
  From the land of my pilgrimage, Welcome me Home.

THE CALL OF THE BRIDEGROOM.

" Till the day break, and the shadows retire."—Cant. iv.

"Till the day break, and the shadows retire,"
Be the flight of the spirit still higher and higher,
Ensnared by no tempter, repelled by no foe,
And forging no fetters to chain her below.

Alone with her Maker the spirit must stand,
Must list to His whisper and lean on His hand,
Must pass through the desert no footstep hath trod,
Till the breath of her perfumes ascends to her God.

"The queens and the maidens" may gather around,
Uncounted in number and brilliantly crowned,
But "one is the chosen" the Monarch doth love,
And His eyes will not suffer a spot in the dove.

Then list to His whisper and wake to His word,
It sounds for whoever its music hath stirred—
"Arise, for the winter is over and gone,
Make haste, for the pruning is yet to come on."

Again, will that whisper sound sweet on the ear—
"Oh! come from Mount Libanus, come without fear,
Oh! come from Amana and look on thy crown,—
Thou hast wounded My Heart, while I aimed at thine own."

"And the stream of strong waters will run from above
To fill thee with torrents of bliss and of love;
For the time is at hand when I grant thy desire—
To see 'the day break, and the shadows retire.'"

"THE NEW AND THE OLD."

"The new and the old, my Beloved, I have kept for Thee."—*Cant.* vii. 13.

Oh! wilt Thou take before I go
    Another gift from me?—
The "New" are all Thine own, I know,
    But so the "Old" should be;
For late acceptance to Thy Throne
    My wandering verses flee;
The fierce are for Thy foes alone,
    The fond are all for Thee.

In those lost days of human zeal,
    When most I went astray,
Thou know'st I did not always feel
    The things I used to say;
But if I thought heart never loved,
    As poet's warm and free,
It was because I never proved
    What 'twas to worship Thee.

And for each fierce defiance hurled,
    Each mocking word of mine,
I cast them at a sinful world
    At war with love divine.

And oh! with all my strength, I pray
   That my old comrades see
And find, in some sweet, future day,
   What 'tis to worship Thee.

THE OFFERING.

O my Love! my Life! my Lord!
Bless the re-awakened chord,
   Vowed at last to Thee.

Give my words the power to sow
Seeds of love where'er they go,
   Preaching far and free.

Bless these songs, for they are Thine
In every thought and every line
   Where love or light may be

But where the thought in vain appeals,
Or where the word the thought conceals,
   The fault is all in me:

Yet, should my pleadings fail to move
The breasts which Thou hast formed to love,
   Oh! be not wroth with me;

For this poor heart that can but sing
Would gladly give its blood to bring
   One erring soul to Thee.

INDEX OF POEMS,

ARRANGED ACCORDING TO SUBJECTS.

ON THE BLESSED SACRAMENT.

	PAGE
Before the Blessed Sacrament	22
Daily Communion	91
To the Lamp before the Blessed Sacrament	95
My God and my All	101
Our best Friend	132
Harbour the Harbourless	174
The Tabernacle	184

ON OUR BLESSED LADY.

Mother all pure	27
The Name of Mary	26
Queen of the Most Holy Rosary	35
Jesus and Mary	44
The Prophecy of Simeon	48
The Flight into Egypt	75
A Word for Holy Images	82
May Wreaths	103
Salus Infirmorum	115
Why do we kneel to Her?	119
The Loss of the Child Jesus	128
Mother of Mercy	150
Mother of Christ	195
Mourn for the Holy Images	206
Queen of Martyrs	230
The Royal Name of Mary	233
Assumption Morning	240
Mother of God	250
Mary is our Queen	259
Our Lady of the Sacred Heart	267
Queen of all Saints	290

ON THE ANGELS.

	PAGE
To my Guardian Angel	21
The Angels	29
Comfort for my Angel	42
Our Elder Brothers	59
Angels of Strength	74
What my Angel could do for me	86
Intercession of the Thrones	106
For my dear Music-Masters	124
The Angel Guide	139
The Angel-Keepers	175
To the Rebuking Angels	214
To Saint Raphael	226
A Hymn for October	250
The Wings of my Angel	270
Our Constant Companions	285

ON THE SAINTS.

	PAGE
1. My own Saint Alphonsus	25
2. A Petition to Saint Alphonsus	88
3. To Saint Alphonsus on my Twenty-sixth Birthday	162
4. Meeting Saint Alphonsus in Heaven	287
1. Saint Dominic	33
2. The Vigils of Saint Dominic	133
3. The Prayer of Father Dominic	237
4. My Prayer to Saint Dominic	284
Saint Agnes	40
1. Twofold Martyrdom	45
2. Saint Sebastian	257
1. Saint Thomas of Aquin	52
2. The Angelic Doctor	222
1. My Prayer to Saint Teresa	62
2. Saint Teresa watching the Blessed Sacrament	208
1. Saint Lewis and the Flowers	67
2. The Dreams of Saint Lewis	245
Saint Joseph	71
1. The Defence in the Hall	76
2. Magdalen's Love	225
Sainted Sisters	103
Saint Pius V.	112
Music on the Mountain	116
The Shrine of Saint James	118
The Contest	120
Saint Alexius	142
The Legend of Blessed Imelda	151
To the Heart of Saint Philip Neri	176
The Vision of Saint Agnes of Montepulciano	182
Mary and Martha	183
Saint Wilfrid and Rome	186
Saint Rose and her Flowers	195
The Curé d'Ars	202
Servants of Mary	210
Father Louis da Ponte	215

				PAGE
Saint Elizabeth of Hungary	...	...	...	218
Blessed James of Mevania	...	...	...	227
Snow Wreaths	...	...	...	264
Blessed Maria Bartholomæa	...	...	...	271
Work for Saint Patrick	...	...	...	273
Varieties	...	...	...	288
The Communion of Saints	...	...	...	123
The Secret of the Saints	...	...	...	213
Saints and Sinners	...	...	...	97

POEMS RELATING TO THE PERSONAL HISTORY OF THE AUTHOR.

A Prayer for the truant Gift of Song	...	...	...	17
To the greater Glory of God	...	...	...	18
Light and Shade	...	...	...	24
Holy Spells	...	...	...	32
Vocation	...	...	...	36
Sisters Three	...	...	...	38
Come back to me	...	...	...	41
Light through Darkness	...	...	...	49
The Minstrel's Gift	...	...	...	50
The Voice of the Sanctuary	...	...	...	65
Names at Confirmation	...	...	...	69
Freedom	...	...	...	75
Breathing Time	...	...	...	84
Spiritual Scenery	...	...	...	93
Hero Worship	...	...	...	100
On the Death of a Young Friend	...	...	...	107
Darkest before Dawn	...	...	...	109
Daily Bread	...	...	...	111
Cries to God	...	...	...	125
Gold or Lead	...	...	...	133
My Holy Beads and Medals Blest	...	...	...	145
Love's Trials	...	...	...	157
Shifting Scenes	...	...	...	159
The Outlaw	...	...	...	164
Night and Morning	...	...	...	189
Our Living Rosary	...	...	...	190
The Answering Picture	...	...	...	199
Solitude	...	...	...	210
Comfort	...	...	...	217
Darkness	...	...	...	227
My Three Acts	...	...	...	229
Weeds and Flowers	...	...	...	232
Home-Sickness	...	...	...	239
The Bell	...	...	...	243
Hope Deferred	...	...	...	244
Beads from the Holy Sepulchre	...	...	...	254
Disappointment	...	...	...	256

	PAGE
My Times are in Thy Hand	258
The Particular Judgment	262
Extreme Unction	262
The Lasting Treasure	266
Blessings	267
Solace for the Weak	269
Home	275
Night-Thoughts	283
Love's Yearnings	286
Upland	291
Foreshadowing	293
Welcome Home	293
The New and the Old	295
The Offering	296

MISCELLANEOUS.

Heaven	19
Hope	25
Look Forward	27
Forget me not	31
The Days when we were Happy	37
All for God	38
Forgive me	39
In earnest	42
Night Watching	43
The Cross	46
The Daisy and the Rose	47
Devotedness	51
"All to all"	56
The Poor	57
Thine and Mine	60
The branch of Green Palms and the Crown of Red Roses	60
The Sun-Dial	61
The Ten Commandments	64
Shadows on our Path	66
Past and Present	69
Pure Gold for the Shrine	72
A cry in Temptation	73
When to Surrender and when to hold fast	77
The Gift for the Giver	78
The Spanish Lady	79
The Lost Talisman	85
The Mercy of God	89
Nature's Book	92
The Legacy	93
All for Love	96
The Stranger	108
The Sun-flower	108
The Withered Flower	114
Fireworks	117
The Power of Art	123

Hope for the Valiant	127
The old Church at Lismore	128
The Sweetness of serving God	131
Fiat	131
Choose Wisely	135
The Sacraments	135
Desolation	139
Laurels Won	140
The Royal Way of the Cross	141
A Cure for Sadness	144
Ballad Songs for the People	147
Angels and Birds	149
Feast of the Transfiguration	149
A Parent's Prayer	154
The Treasure of Love	155
Dewdrops on Thorns	156
Our Holy Mother the Church	160
Aspiration	161
Remember Me	161
Verses for every hour in the Day	165
Light on the Hill-top	172
Mount Thabor	172
Swan-like	174
God in All	176
"Taste and See"	177
The Valiant Woman	178
Everything for Thee	180
Defence	181
Taking Sanctuary	181
To my Creator	189
The Crucifix	191
An Act of Homage	192
Confidence	193
England	194
Phases of Love	196
Church Flowers	198
"Thy Will be done"	200
Cross and Crown	204
Viaticum	205
Fetters	207
Lines written in Blessed Henry Suso's "Little Book of Eternal Wisdom"	211
Sunshine through Showers	215
The Meeting	221
Festival Ground	223
Strength before Sweetness	231
Eternity transmutes	234
The Welcome Visitor	235
The Ways of God	238
A Song of the easons	241
Hours of Idleness	242
Wishes	243
The Lily among Thorns	248
The Last Combat	248

	PAGE
Final Perseverance	255
Homeward Bound	255
Prayer	259
White Lilies	261
A Premium for Silence	265
Music worth waiting for	274
The Presentation Nun	276
Charitas	278
A Legend of Melleraye	279
The Call of the Bridegroom	294

THE END.

Printed by M. H. Gill & Son, 50 Upper Sackville-st., Dublin.

www.ingramcontent.com/pod-product-compliance
Lightning Source LLC
Chambersburg PA
CBHW022050230426
43672CB00008B/1127